To Vern:

Morris Chalfen sent me to Detroit in 1947 with a check for $15,000 and I came home with the Gems franchise from the struggling National Basketball League. The failed Gems team became the Minneapolis Lakers. We won the title in the NBL in our first season.

We were one of four teams that moved to the Basketball Association of America, winning that championship in 1949. The league then changed its name to the National Basketball Association. One of the best centers coming out of college basketball that fall was Hamline's Vern Mikkelsen. The NBA had a territorial draft that year and the Lakers took Mikkelsen, having the rights to any player in a team's region in the first round.

Mikkelsen was a great kid out of Askov, a small Minnesota town. His only problem was that he was too nice. If he knocked a guy to the court he would apologize. But he became a fine player for the Lakers, entering the starting lineup. Mikkelsen did not have an outside shot, playing through high school and college with his back to the basket. Teams would sag in on George Mikan. They would let Vern stand wide open. Mikkelsen began to work on an overhead, two-handed outside shot. He became almost deadly from 15 feet.

The Lakers won four titles in five years with the Mikan-Mikkelsen-Jim Pollard combination up front. Vern was the first power forward. He believed that he never fouled anybody, but officials thought otherwise.

One of my last acts in helping Laker ownership was attempting to trade Vern to Boston. It was half-way through the 1955-56 season and we were going nowhere. The Celtics needed a center. I planned to trade Vern to them for three University of Kentucky players (including Cliff Hagan) who were in the service. Most important, I believed that trading Vern to Boston would insure us of finishing last. That would give us a chance to draft Bill Russell. Owner Ben Berger backed out of the deal.

When George Mikan started having his severe health problems in 1995, no one showed more concern and made such an effort to spend time with him as Vern did, showing us again that he was still the great person from the small town who first showed up at Hamline. When you add it up, player and person, we haven't had many better in all my years in sports than Vern Mikkelsen.

– Sid Hartman

THE
VERN MIKKELSEN
STORY

Vern Mikkelsen

HOF '95

THE VERN

MIKKELSEN STORY

STORY

The Original Power Forward

John
Egan

NODIN PRESS

Acknowledgements: John Kundla, Janice Egan, Pat and George Mikan, Howie Schultz, Keith Paisley, Carl Bennett, Charles Erickson, Norton Stillman, Joe Hutton Jr., Basketball Hall of Fame, Dana Johnson of Hamline University, Dan Benson of the University of North Dakota, Lute Olson, Arilee Pollard, Dean Belbas, Rob Lahammer, Dave Strain, Ken Thompson, Rollie Seltz, John Mikkelsen, Dan Loritz, Jack Schmid, Jodie Flolid.

Photos from the Mikkelsen, Mikan, and Pollard family collections; drawings by George Karn, Phil Bissell, and Bob Parker.

ISBN 13: 978-1-932472-43-1
ISBN 10: 1-932472-43-6
Library of Congress Control Number: 2006932127

design and layout: John Toren
front cover: Mark Herman

Nodin Press is a division of Micawbers, Inc.
530 North Third Street
Suite 120
Minneapolis, MN 55401

When the Minneapolis lakers dominated the NBA, it was common knowledge that Vern Mikkelsen played a crucial role in their enormous success. He wasn't a flashy player. He did much of the hard, tough work that it takes to win championships— rebounding, starting fast breaks, defense, and setting picks for others to get shots. He was able to do those things yet still score enough crucial points to help win almost all their games. He was a great player, and he is a great person. This book will be an inspiration to anyone regarding how they should approach their lives and careers.

– Bill Sharman, Boston Celtics guard and
Basketball Hall of Famer as both player and coach

In the Middle Ages of pro basketball, the 1950s, there was an athlete who might have sat at Camelot's Round Table. He was an unselfish, decent man, Vem Mikkelsen. But when he leaped for a rebound or drove to the basket, bones crunched, the glass shook and his team, the Lakers, invariably won. Without heraldry he became a figure of basketball history, the first of the great power forwards. His story is one today's generation of basketball wonks need to know. It's told with pace, respect and humor by a fine writer, John Egan.

– Jim Klobuchar,
newspaper columnist and author

We put in a play for Vern called 'The Askov.' He was to set a pick here, set a pick there. And Vern asked me, 'Then what?' I told him 'Then you go over and get the rebound.'

– John Kundla, Laker coach

It took Mik about four years to grow into the full potential of the power forward position he created, and to perfect it. Actually, he was pretty darn good at it right from the start. It was a bruising business in there, but I think he enjoyed it. Heck, I know he enjoyed it. The rougher it got the wider his smile.

– George Mikan

Vern, you've created a position [power forward] in which you have to be a combination weight lifter, safe cracker, and basketball player.

– Bill Carlson, *Minneapolis Star* sports reporter during the Lakers' Minneapolis era

I said I'd call off the deal if Mikkelsen does not want to go. And he told me he doesn't.

– Ben Berger, owner of the Lakers, on the occasion of trade talks that would have sent Vern Mikkelsen to Boston for Frank Ramsey, Cliff Hagan, and Lou Tsioropoulos in 1956

Even to those of us on another side of sports, Vern was known as just a great, great guy. Last time I was with him he was troubled by aching hips but still had that gracious, friendly way about him.

– Jim Perry, Twins pitcher and Cy Young award winner in 1970

CONTENTS

LAKERS TIMELINE

1947 — Lakers are formed, Pollard from the beginning, Mikan after four games, Kundla coach

1948 — Champion of National Basketball League (not recognized by the NBA)

1949 — Champion of Basketball Association of America (recognized by the NBA)

1950 — NBA Champions; Mikan and rookie Mikkelsen play 68 games, Pollard 66

1951 — Winner of NBA Western Division; runner-up to Rochester in finals as Mikan plays despite ankle fracture

1952 — NBA Champions

1953 — NBA Champions

1954 — NBA Champions; Mikan retires

1955 — Lost in Western Division finals; Pollard retires

1956 — Lost in Western Division semifinals; Mikan returns for final 37 games

1957 — Lost in Western Division semifinals

1959 — Runner up to Boston in NBA finals; Mikkelsen retires, Kundla takes University of Minnesota coaching job

1960 — Team departs for Los Angeles

INTRODUCTION

Bob Pettit

Few basketball players in the history of the game have had the spectacular success enjoyed by Bob Pettit. In 69 games of collegiate competition at Louisiana State University, the 6-foot-9 200-pound All-American from Baton Rouge averaged just under 28 points and 11 rebounds a game. During an 11-year career (starting as a No. 1 draft pick in 1954) with the Milwaukee/ Saint Louis Hawks, he was Rookie of the Year in the National Basketball Association and played in 11 All-Star Games. He averaged 26 points a game and was named to the Basketball Hall of Fame in 1970. He was the NBA's Most Valuable Player in 1956 and 1959 and led the Hawks to the NBA title in 1958. He retired in 1965 as the leading scorer in NBA history and its second leading rebounder.

Pettit was selected by Mikkelsen to be his presenter at the former Minneapolis Laker's Hall of Fame induction in 1995. The two earliest of power forwards had epic battles during the five years when their careers overlapped.

This is what Pettit says about his former basketball foe:

I have the utmost respect for Vern Mikkelsen both as a basketball player and a person. I am honored to participate in this manner in the telling of my friend's life story.

Vern was an extremely fine player, played on a very fine team. I caught him during the last half of his career, the first half of mine. During those five years, he demonstrated to me, often quite forcefully, what it means to be a fierce competitor every second you are on the basketball floor.

Vern was the epitome of big, strong—yes "power"—forward. He was a terrific rebounder, a good defensive player, and used an exceptional two-handed set shot from outside. The latter kept defenders like me "honest" as we had to cover him outside and under.

I can laugh about it now, but Vern beat me to death, just as he did everybody else, I'm sure. But he seemed to take particular pleasure in working over my skinny body.

There was no way that I, or anyone else, was going to intimidate him. He was able to hold his position against any of us. I'm sure he did that from the first game he ever played in a Laker uniform, yielding the center position for the Lakers to the incomparable George Mikan while moving out to a new spot facing the basket.

When I would venture into the pivot, his answer was to send me flying out to midcourt. He was nice about it though. If I was knocked to the court, he'd smile and pick me up.

Let me say this in the most complimentary way possible. I am sure that he liked pounding on me more than any other player. I took it as a sign of the respect he must have had for me.

I considered it a great honor to present him at his Basketball Hall of Fame induction in 1995. I get the same feeling now as I help bring Vern's story to the world. Because he played somewhat in the shadow of two such all-time stars as Jim Pollard and George Mikan, not nearly enough is known about this great basketball player and first-class person. This book will do much to correct that misfortune.

PREFACE

by Vern Mikkelsen

The desk I currently work from is the same desk on which my dad, a Danish Lutheran Minister, used to write his sermons some 70 odd years ago. When I was just 3 or 4 years old I would sit beneath the snug cubby of this very desk while my Dad hovered above me writing, puffing on his pipe—it was surely the safest I've felt my entire life. Now 70 years later, a similar security pervades my soul as I sit writing at the same desk.

The book you're holding in your hands is the story of my life and career. But there is little greatness to be found in throwing a ball through a hoop. I was a good basketball player, but I attribute greatness to those individuals who sacrifice their time, talents, and efforts for the benefit of others. I did some of that, too, though not nearly as much as I would have liked to, looking back on it. All the same, I very much appreciate the admiration and honor I continue to receive half a century after retiring from the sport I still enjoy watching, and enjoyed playing competitively over a twenty-year span of time. Entertaining and inspiring people also contributes to the quality of their lives, I guess.

I am blessed to have lived a long life with some interesting highlights along the way. A few of those highlights have been gathered here. Most of them concern my days with the Minneapolis Lakers. The stories have been organized and put into narrative form by the author, my friend John Egan. But I'd like to say a few words about how the stories got recorded in the first place.

Sometime before my wife died in 2002, I suffered a severe stroke. The unfamiliar environment in which my body and mind found themselves was one where I could still think thoughts, but couldn't speak them or write them out. My doctor made it known almost immediately that the most important component of my recovery would be my attitude toward the work required to regain my speech habits. Sure, medication would help, but the doctor made it clear that it would largely be up to me, supported by my faith in God, to work as hard as I could if I wanted to make my remaining years good ones. When I attempted to communicate with him using a clumsy movement of my hand that I wanted to write—I couldn't even write my own name at that point—he encouraged me that writing would help, though he suggested doing crosswords and other mind-motor exercises as a start. I wanted to do more.

What ensued was a challenge I embraced and actually began looking forward to every day. I started writing down simple memorable experiences from my life - the ones that brought the most joy. Next thing I knew I had graduated from learning how to write my name again to filling up a pile of yellow legal pads with memories and anecdotes from seventy-five years of my life.

As my newfound desire for writing continued and my stroke symptoms dissipated, my string of health-related chal- lenges grew. But they were no longer nearly as daunting, now that the writing had given me something to look forward to every day—and I might say, to live for. Even if my notes were never read by anyone, it didn't matter—the writing was healing and provided peace of mind. It wasn't until my two sons Tom and John encouraged me to publish my notes that I ever considered the possibility. It simply wasn't my intention.

Having weathered two botched hip replacements, prostate cancer, diabetes, hearing loss, two strokes, and the loss of sight in one eye, I now live thankfully day to day. Whew! What a disheartening roster to claim as your own! I share the details of my recent health issues not for sympathy but to inspire those suffering mentally or physically not to lose hope. Keep on doing your best with what you have to work with, as we all have an obligation to take care of ourselves and live as long as possible, respecting each day as a great gift with the intention of sharing the simple, meaningful things of life with family, friends and our community. I encourage you to find something you love to do and commit to doing that thing every day. Find the thing that brings joy—to you and to others—and get at it! "It's not how much you do, but how much Love you put into the doing, that matters…"

My son John has recently come back from Los Angeles to stay with me, and we remind each other every day how grateful we are "to have received another one,"—another day that is. So very many did not wake up this morning, be grateful you have.

I believe that had I not suffered a stroke I might never have experienced this wonderful, unforeseen process of developing the material for a book. My stroke, ironically, gave me something to live for. We truly can turn an adversity into a positive experience if we so choose—I'm living proof.

Thank you for picking up my story, I hope you enjoy reading the memoirs of a small town kid who was so very fortunate to be taught by his parents that friends, family and faith are the three most important things in life—and to treat them as such.

Here's to Friends, Family & Faith!

Sincerely,

Vern Mikkelsen

Special Thanks to my wife of 47 years, Jean, my sons Tom and John, daughter-in-law Jennifer, two grandsons Kyler and Caden, Jim Jackson & family, Jean Davis & family, John Egan, Norton Stillman & Nodin Press, Linda Rambis and the entire Los Angeles Lakers Organization, The Minnesota Diabetes Foundation, Bill Austin & The Starkey Hearing Foundation, The Willmatt Hill Crew and Breconwood friends, The Naismith Hall of Fame—and last but certainly not least, my dear friends at Hamline University.

A percentage of the proceeds from this book will go to The Minnesota Diabetes Foundation and The Starkey Hearing Foundation.

> *With love*
> *I dedicate this book*
> *to my*
> *Mom and Dad*

Prologue

It was two days after Thanksgiving, 1949. Grunts and groans were emanating from the gym at the Minneapolis Athletic Club. Sneakers squeaked across the wooden floor, balls banged off rims, wet bodies jolted against one another.

The kings of professional basketball were working out under the scrutiny of Coach John Kundla, as he tinkered with his new, experimental "double post" offense. Suddenly the voice of George Mikan boomed above the basketball din:

"It's too darn crowded in here."

Mikan had become exasperated by the cramped quarters as he and Mikkelsen jostled with their two defenders within the narrow confines of a six-foot free-throw lane.

Coach Kundla agreed, and another trial began.

In 1949 the Minneapolis Lakers were champions of the basketball world. It hardly seemed time for a radical change. Yet the personnel Kundla had at his disposal seemed to call for a new configuration. Kundla moved Mikkelsen out to the right forward position, facing the basket on offense for the first time in his competitive life. With Jim Pollard on the left and Mikan in the middle, a new style of basketball was born. So was a new position—Power Forward.

By New Year's Day of 1950 the National Basketball Association was witnessing the effects of the bold change. The Lakers were better than ever! Other teams soon began to imitate the new configuration, but it would be several years before anyone challenged the Lakers' dominance on the court. Basketball had been changed forever. And Mikkelsen's legend was assured.

– John Egan

1

It Must be a Dream

There I was with George Mikan, Elgin Baylor, Sha-quille O'Neal and Kobe Bryant! Kobe and Shaq, the two young superstars, couldn't have been more gracious as we chatted in the Staples Center about the common love of the game of basketball we all shared. I had to ask myself, "What am I doing here with four of the greatest athletes of all time?" I was certain that any moment I would be awakened by my mom back home in Askov, Minnesota, just another twelve-year-old kid getting ready to go to school!

I truly thought I must be dreaming.

*   *   *   *   *   *   *

When I, John Egan, met Vern Mikkelsen a year later, I reassured him that the meeting in Los Angeles which seemed so remarkable to him had actually taken place. (On April 11, 2002, to be precise.) It wasn't a figment of his imagination, and furthermore, no one belonged in that elite crowd more than he did. Gathered were the Old Lakers—the Minneapolis team that had won a string of three NBA championships between 1952 and

3

1955—and the New Lakers, who had brought two straight National Basketball Association championships to Los Angeles, and would wrap up a third later that spring.

After the meeting with Shaq and Kobe (who were on their way to a halftime session with Coach Phil Jackson), Mikkelsen was called to center court along with Mikan and Baylor for a special celebration. (Seven months later, members of the Minneapolis championship teams received giant, diamond-encrusted rings identical to the ones the "new" Lakers had just earned by winning another NBA championship.) At the ceremony banners with numbers signifying years and players rose to the rafters, and cheers filled the auditorium from floor to ceiling. Two "families" were being joined into one. It was a unique and remarkable moment in basketball history.

Mikkelsen, a small town boy and son of a Danish Lutheran pastor, remembers it as if it were yesterday: "Each of us old-timers had been assigned a 'sponsor.' Elgin was with George; James Worthy was with me; Jerry West with Slater Martin; Mitch Kupchak with Jim Pollard's widow, Arilee; Bill Sharman with our coach John Kundla, and Magic Johnson with Clyde Lovellette. Yes, I think it is understandable that I sat there almost numb, wondering what I could possibly have done to be included with some of the greatest players ever to pull on a pair of basketball sneakers. Phil Jackson, too, was a good player himself who became a highly successful coach.

"When I told friend John Egan about it in one of our many brunch and lunch sessions beginning about a year later, I said that a small-town Minnesotan like me couldn't actually have been a part of such an awesome affair. My respect for the game was such that I figured it must be a mistake."

As a sports journalist with an acute sense of basketball legend, I continued the job of convincing Vern that his career deserved such recognition, that he belonged at courtside chatting and exchanging handshakes with Hollywood celebrities such as Jack Nicholson, Penny Marshall, and Dyan Cannon.

Mikkelsen chokes up when telling of tears shed while exchanging hugs with Elgin Baylor, an NBA rookie during Mikkelsen's last Laker season in Minneapolis.

One of the points Mikkelsen emphasizes when he describes his dramatic life is the role played by "family" in many aspects of it—a huge example being the gathering of young and old Lakers standing shoulder to shoulder.

The Lakers, that night at the Staples Center, were wearing vintage uniforms from the Minneapolis era, with MPLS embroidered conspicuously across the front. The NBA had recently replicated these throwback uniforms to market to a new generation of fans, many of whom had not been aware that the Laker franchise got its start in Minneapolis. It caused Mikan to remark, "It's great that the NBA is finally recognizing us old guys."

My own memories of the trail-blazing Lakers go back to their earliest years, and as a seasoned minstrel, I know a powerful story when I see it. Talking with Vern during the months after that memorable night at the Staples Center, it was clear to me that I'd found one.

2

The Reverie Begins

Like many young parents, the Reverend Michael Mikkelsen and his wife Elna were full of joy and hope on October 21, 1928, when a son, whom they named Arild Verner Agerskov Mikkelsen, was born to them in the sleepy town of Parlier in California's Central Valley. Certainly no one in the Reverend's congregation assembled at the Danish Lutheran Church or his sister church in nearby Easton a few days later could have guessed that the squirming new arrival they were gazing down upon would one day become the original power forward and change the way Americans play the game of basketball forever.

Six months later Vern's father, who had been a pastor in Easton, accepted a call to the Nazareth Lutheran Church in Withee, Wisconsin, some forty miles east of Eau Claire. For Reverend Mikkelsen this move was what we would call a lateral one, for money was scarce and his new congregation could best pay the pastor in chickens, eggs, butter, and pigs. But there are more important things in life than money, and the Reverend's passion for worshipping God in a Danish setting was insatiable.

The family spent seven and a half years in Withee. The most dramatic moment for Vern was when a teacher named

The Mikkelsens in Parlier, California, 1929

Louise Hansen decided to advance him a grade. That put him in a grade with youngsters a year or two older (he had started first grade at age five). He was to be in the "younger" element in many aspects of his life thereafter. "It was not that I was that smart," Mikkelsen says now of the grade skip, self-effacing as usual. "It was a financial move for the school, which saved money because they actually were able to clear an entire grade by moving two people." By most any standards, that reflects a small enrollment. Vern, however, was to be in a succession of small schools.

Vern's first recollections of his youth go back to the time spent in Withee alongside the Black River west of town. "I can remember my folks taking us three kids there to go swimming." Many years later Vern and his sister Hertha returned to the church where their father had served for its one-hundredth anniversary. "Louise Hansen, my former teacher, was still playing the organ at the church though ninety-some years old," Vern said.

On October 21, 1936, Vern's eighth birthday, Reverend Mikkelsen moved his family to Dagmar, Montana, to serve a church there as well as a sister Danish Lutheran congregation a few miles away at Volmar. The Mikkelsens resided seven miles west of the North Dakota state line, twenty-five miles south of the Canadian border. Sister Esther, six years older than Vern, went to high school as a freshman in Medicine Lake, fifteen miles southwest on the edge of the Fort Peck Indian Reservation. She stayed in town with friends of the Mikkelsens.

Vern as a baby with his mother and sisters

Vern and his other sister, Hertha, who was four years older than him, went to elementary school in Dagmar.

In the spring of 1938, the Mikkelsens' nine-year-old boy entered the Sheridan County Roundup athletic events. "I made my mom very proud," he later recalled, by finishing first in his class at various skills. (This was the first time the word "champion" was used in reference to him.) He had still not seen his first basketball … nine years old and growing fast.

Of northeast Montana, Vern recalls the hardscrabble land and the persistent drought. "My mom almost gave up shortly after we moved there when a wicked sandstorm blew through, leaving us with a house full of sand and dust that took two weeks to clean up."

The Medicine Lake National Wildlife Refuge sat in the middle of a huge expanse of wheat growers. "Many farms were full-section size," Vern says. "But lack of rainfall ruined the farmers." Reverend Mikkelsen often traveled east to serve a church at Flaxton, North Dakota, a tiny Danish community across the state line. He also went up into the borderlands of Canada to assist Danish congregations there.

Reverend Mikkelsen was not fond of the school system at Dagmar, and a planned Danish "folk school" did not materialize, so the family again packed its bags. Reverend Mikkelsen had asked for and received a transfer from Montana (where the nearest town of any size was Williston, North Dakota, fifty miles to the southeast) to another Danish hamlet. He turned down an offer of a section of land if he'd stay as a pastor-farmer, and in the summer of 1939, the Mikkelsens moved to Askov, Minnesota, some fifty miles south of Duluth near the western tip of Lake Superior. That fall, young Mikkelsen was introduced to basketball.

Or rather, basketball was introduced to him.

Welcome to Basketball

"My first time in the Askov gym, there were guys playing hoops. I asked if I could play, and they said sure. I grabbed the ball and raced toward a basket. They all started to holler at me. 'Traveling!' Those shouts were my baptism to the game. I had no idea what I was doing. But I learned quickly enough."

Learning basketball helped Vern overcome the disappointment of leaving his friends behind in scorching, bone-dry Montana, and before long Vern had become extremely happy in Askov. "Faith in God and love of family already were helping me make adjustments," he said.

While Vern was moving through Askov's seventh and eighth grades, a huge influence on his life was the school superintendent, Otto Hoiberg. Hoiberg helped Mikkelsen with some of the nuances of basketball (starting with dribbling instead of just running with the ball).

Hoiberg, who died in February, 2004, at age 95, followed his protégé's basketball career throughout high school, on into college, and finally with the Lakers. "And, I," Vern says, "followed with great interest the basketball accomplishments of Otto's grandson, Fred Hoiberg, through high school in Ames, Iowa, then Iowa State, and on to the pros with the Pacers, Bulls, and Minnesota Timberwolves. Otto and my dad, both Danish, stayed great friends, even after Otto moved to Lincoln, Nebraska, to pursue a career in education."

Askov, a community of 350 residents (99 percent of them Danish), was the first town the Mikkelsens lived in where Vern could travel about on his own. He says he was "a good boy and stayed out of trouble. Had to!"

Askov was about four blocks long and five blocks wide with the Great Northern Railroad running through south to north, parallel to Main Street. Bethlehem Lutheran Church and the brick parsonage were one and a half blocks east of the tracks. Hans Christian Andersen High School (named after the Dane who wrote fairy tales including "The Little Mermaid," "The Red Shoes," "The Ugly Duckling," and "The Brave Tin Soldier") was one and a half blocks west of the tracks alongside the Danish Brotherhood Society building, which was the scene of various gatherings including dances on Saturday night. "Dad wasn't happy with those, and I didn't go," Vern says.

Three miles west of Askov was the Kettle River, where Vern often fished with family or friends. Surrounding the town were rutabaga fields—the rocky ground in that region of Minnesota seemed unsuitable for much else. The uncrowned but actual King of the Rutabagas was Andrew Hendricksen. He was an enterprising Dane who, particularly during World War II, cruised the region in his big Pontiac and lined up significant sales of the edible, yellowish variety of turnip (often called, to the disgust of Askov folks, the "Swedish turnip"). When he was twelve and thirteen, Vern delivered the *Minneapolis Star* on a route of some twenty subscribers.

Vern fishing with his dad

In a community not blessed with refinements such as streetlights, Askov thrived on activities evolving out of the high school and the Danish Brotherhood Society. Civic functions were carried on some twenty-eight miles south at Pine City, the Pine County seat.

The Rutabaga Festivals were summer highlights, but in wintertime interest in Askov turned to the exploits of the high school boys basketball team, nicknamed the Danes, of course. Hans Christian Andersen school through consolidation has been changed to a junior high. (Mikkelsen's No. 99 jersey from his high school basketball days can still be seen in the glass display case.)

Though the main artery past Askov is now Interstate 35, "in my day it was U.S. Highway 61," Vern says. "Ran all the way from Duluth to New Orleans." That highway was just west of Askov across the Kettle River bridge.

Askov was only twenty-five miles west of the Wisconsin border. The Danes' basketball team found competition to the north and south. Askov played teams from Pine City (the largest area town by far), Barnum, Moose Lake, Sandstone, Finlayson, Willow River, Hinckley, and even Bruno, which had no actual gymnasium.

"They then used a classroom that had baskets as a court," Vern recalls. "The desks were moved so that we could play there despite a low ceiling that was only about as high as the top of a backboard. We once beat Bruno 7 to 6 in a game we talked about for a long time.

"Pine City beat us out in the District 25 finals when I was a senior. Les Nell, the coach at Pine City, became a great friend after that, and he hardly ever failed to pull out that scorebook when I stopped to visit. After I joined the Lakers, I sometimes took summer trips for the organization to sell game tickets. I would visit Les and get the names of the key person that every town has in that regard."

In 1940, when Vern was in eighth grade, Askov High applied some Danish magic to District 25 by winning the championship. The Danes defeated Lindstrom-Center City in the finals 32-23 after first ousting Hinckley 45-39 and then North Branch 26-22 in the semifinals. "The Pine City auditorium was packed for the finals," said an *Askov American* account of the triumph. "Going through a tough schedule of games, the boys, for the first time, brought to Askov two beautiful trophies as symbols of championship honor, both in the sub-district and the district. North Branch finished third."

Vern remembers, "Those guys were my first sports heroes. Fred Degerstrom, who was captain, and Coach Harold Jensen. And Arden Hyldahl, Carl Sandahl, Jens Lund, Roger Sorensen, Carl Hansen, Marvin Jensen, and Harry Mortensen."

Mikkelsen began play-

A 15-year-old Vern in Askov, September 1944

ing as a regular for Askov High as a freshman. Because he was always the tallest player, he was at the center position from the start. Playing his entire high school and college career with his back to the basket caused some concern later in his athletic life, but no one considered those possibilities then. "I was pushing 6-foot-5 by the time I was sixteen," Vern says. "I was a senior that year, and we had a very good team. By then I was wearing No. 99, oddly the number George Mikan was to wear later with us Lakers."

The Danes lost to Pine City 41-36 in the opening game of the 1945 district tournament after defeating Willow River, Sandstone, and Barnum in the north-half sub-district. The Pine City loss was the team's first after 17 straight wins. Mikkelsen led the team in scoring for the season with 215 points. Captain Norman ("Bake") Christensen contributed 124 points and Byron ("Bud") Petersen, who was 6-foot-2, scored 111. The team was a tall one for that era, averaging 6-foot-1 through the squad of nine. Tom Thomsen, Hans Abrahamsen, and Dwain Thomsen also played significant roles for Coach Theodore C. Sjoding. Ray Olesen, Jim Pearson and Glen Mortensen rounded out the roster. "We had wanted to at least equal what the 1940 team had done. Roger "Stumpy" Sorensen [who later taught both of Vern's sons, Tom and John, in Hopkins, Minnesota] and that bunch got to the regional before being eliminated. But we fell short in what we thought was an upset."

Mikkelsen says, "It was no big deal in those days being a regular as a freshman. I was tallest and we didn't have that many boys in school. I was in the band all those years, too. Had to jump up onto the stage [alongside the court] and play, dressed in my basketball stuff. Then hop down to the floor at the start of the game. It was something my Laker teammates thought was quite funny when they heard about it. There were never enough kids so I was in three straight senior class plays, as a sophomore, junior, and then senior. Matter of fact, in later years it would amuse people when I would tell them that I was fourth academically in my Askov class, but I was not in the top third. There were only

Vern with teammates Jim Pearson and Glen "Buzz" Mortenson

nine students in my class!" Through those years, Mikkelsen worked for farmers near Askov to make spending money, pulling "roots" (rutabagas).

In Mikkelsen's high school annual it was announced that he spent at least a bit of class time "arguing with teachers" and whistling. "Mickey," "Joe," and "Butch" were his high school nicknames. The class prophecy proved to be amazingly accurate: "What should we see in New York City near Madison Square Garden but a statue of Verner Mikkelsen, tallest and best basketball player in the world. When we walked past a fieldhouse we saw Mickey coaching a group of basketball boys."

In addition to being secretary-treasurer of his class, Vern had basketball, track, and kittenball among his listed activities. There was no football team. He was on the annual staff, as were seven of his classmates. Vern wrote for the school newspaper, acted in plays, and was in boys and mixed chorus as well as the band. His descriptive line—one was assigned to each senior by a committee— was "Argue, argue early and late. If a line be crooked, he'd make it straight." As Vern would joke later, "I can't argue with that."

On the basketball page of his annual, in addition to a squad picture, there was a picture of a smiling Vern with arms outstretched from his sides, "palming" a ball in each hand. Pearson and Mortensen stood their tallest, the tops of their heads barely reaching the elbows of No. 99. Each of the three wore the knee pads and knee-length striped socks of the day, black basketball shoes, and "short" shorts. A backboard with basket was attached to the brick wall behind them. It was testimony to the joy of small-town basketball before the end of World War II, which Vern had become a part of when his family moved to Askov in 1939.

In addition to all else, Vern was in Boy Scouts, but his pursuit of the Eagle rank was cut short when he went off to college at Hamline University at the tender age of sixteen.

In 1995, as he was about to be inducted into the National Basketball Hall of Fame at Springfield, Massachusetts, Mikkelsen was asked to be grand marshal of the August parade in Askov. He had been dealing with considerable pain because of hip surgery at the time, and asked how long he might be riding in what for the 6-foot-7 ex-Laker would be rather tight quarters in the back seat of a convertible. "I was told that because Main Street was only a couple of blocks long, we would go around twice. I could handle that."

3

The Big Bang

Al Holst had heard the sounds before. A loud BANG! was followed by a thump, thump, thump. He knew immediately that a tire had blown.

He had left the highway around noon on that hot summer day in 1944, in hopes of getting a bite to eat on the main street in Askov. First, he thought, I've got to get the flat fixed. Strange as it may seem, this simple decision would dramatically alter the history of basketball in the Upper Midwest and, yes, even the history of the National Basketball Association itself.

During the academic year Holst was a professor of education at Hamline University in Saint Paul, but he spent many of his waking summer moments as a recuiter, touring Minnesota and Wisconsin in search of potential Hamline students. If some of them were athletes, all the better.

On that particular day Holst was en route to the Minnesota Iron Range to talk to students in various high schools. He pulled his 1936 coupe into Elmer Morgensen's service station in hopes of getting the tire repaired and was met by Morgensen himself. The two struck up a conversation, and when Morgensen learned what Holst's journey was all about, he lifted a fellow Dane into the mix by saying, "Well, we have a pretty darn good basketball player right here in Askov who will be a senior next fall."

Holst, never one to back away from a recruitment possibility, figured this "Verner" whom Morgensen was touting just might be a good fit for Coach Joe Hutton's program. He asked Morgensen just where this Mikkelsen lad might be found.

Mikkelsen describes what happened next: "Morgensen, looking at his watch, said that afternoon Holst surely would find me in a field four miles east of Askov pulling rutabaga. Al drove out there, and I was seriously impressed. First, he was in a Buick, and you didn't see much in Pine County but Fords and Chevies. He drove right out into the field and stopped by me. He got out and asked if I might be Vern Mikkelsen. I was amazed that this middle-aged man from the city, wearing coat, tie, chapeau, and driving a Buick, actually knew me. He knew *me!*"

Holst started to give Vern the Hamline spiel. "I listened carefully but the two words which stuck in my mind indelibly were 'Methodist school.' To a life-long Lutheran and son of a Danish minister, that seemed especially sinister. I told him that he had better come to our house that evening and talk to my folks. He said that he would, and that he was anxious to show us how this could work.

"I had been gracious at least partly because I was so impressed that someone of Holst's style would know about me. I did not yet know that it was Mr. Morgensen who had recommended me. Holst wanted me. A skinny 6-foot-4 senior-to-be did not expect such treatment in Askov.

"That evening at our house, my dad was skeptical at first, as I had expected. In fact, he took me aside and told me he

The 1944 Askov basketball team.
Vern is in the front row, second from the right.

did not think it would work for me at a Methodist school. Then he told Holst that we did not have much money—an understatement—and added that I was planning to wait a year after high school before even considering college because I needed to raise some money.

"Then Al said something that sounded like free tuition, and my dad's eyebrows raised a little. He took me into the kitchen again and said that he thought I *could* do all right at Hamline even though it was run by Methodists. In fact, he agreed to Holst that we would give it a try. Now I really had another element to tease my thoughts during my senior year in high school. I was going to go to Hamline. I was so glad my dad changed his mind."

Some of Vern's classmates were headed into the armed services after graduation, but Mikkelsen was only sixteen years old. During that final high school year, the Askov locker room, gymnasium, and even the high school halls had a new look. No longer was the future indefinite. Vern was college-bound! The news reverberated through the Mikkelsen family all the way to Danevang, Texas, near Galveston, "where many of my mom's relatives lived. Danes growing cotton." Vern worked hard to improve his basketball skills, and with his teammates' help, the Danes were unbeaten during the regular season, though they succumbed to Pine City in the District 25 opener.

During his senior year Vern continued to tease classmate Ila Mortensen incessantly. Doris Nielsen ignored his whistling to the point that she testified to his being a "swell kid" in the school annual. His "good times" continued with fellow senior Folmer Frederiksen, a friendship so strong that Vern slipped and once called Folmer by his real name when on stage in a school play. The other eight seniors, including teammates Byron Petersen and Raymond Olesen, saw all fourteen regular-season basketball opponents subdued, from Bruno 32-10 in the opener to McGrath 81-35 in the last game prior to sub-district competition. The school annual said that the Danes were "confident but not cocky."

The annual went on to say that "our towering team would have been lost if it had not been for its 'toweringest' player, Verner Mikkelsen, who always got the rebound and piled up a high score for every game.

"At Sandstone in the sub-district tournament, he amazed fellow players and spectators alike by scoring 32 points in one of the smoothest played games of the year against our old basketball enemy, the Panthers," the annual account concluded.

One might suspect that friend Folmer, acknowledged as a bit of a poet and on the annual staff, had a hand in that description. Mikkelsen averaged 15½ points a game.

Another annual note: "The final game in the sub-district was played against Barnum and it was a tough game. The Barnum players were good sports as well as ball handlers and it was a pleasure playing [and winning] against them. [But] the good luck of the Askov five left us in the first district game against Pine City. This was a hard-fought game, but we were unable to hold a lead."

For the season, the Danes averaged 46 points a game to opponents' 25 heading into sub-district competition. Mikkelsen still remembers with a bit of sadness the closing loss to Pine City. "We could have, should have, beat them. But they hung in there and won."

Vern's memories of his Askov days revolve around basketball, naturally, but there is much more. "Many of the sermons my dad preached back then were in Danish. I was confirmed in Danish. Some Danish was spoken on the streets of Askov, and you had to know some to get along."

How did that particular group of young Danes prepare for their glorious senior season? "We were the gym rats of that era," Mikkelsen said. "Talking the superintendent into opening the gym on Saturdays wasn't difficult. After all, Mr. Sjoding also was our coach. It was special, the friendships, the successes, the hard work we did and the enjoyment we had doing it as a true team. The town will always be my home town to me. My parents are buried there, in Bethlehem Cemetery."

But when the summer of 1945 arrived, Askov was filed among Mikkelsen's memories. After all, recollections are what permit visions of jonquils in January and snowballs in July.

Hamline University

And it was time. He actually was on his way to Hamline and a new world.

College Life

Vern remembers vividly the trip south toward the Twin Cities. "Dad drove me down. I remember so much of the trip, like it was yesterday. As we were traveling down Highway 61, Dad stopped in Sandstone for gas. He knew the guy who ran the station, who was in dirty overalls pumping our gas. The station guy saw a Hamline sticker I had put in the car window. He looked at the sticker, looked at my dad, and then looked at me. 'Hey, that's where I went to school,' he said. As we got back onto the highway to continue our trip, Dad looked at me with a smile that was fighting a frown for space on his face. He said he wondered if that guy was typical of Hamline products. I think he had something else in mind for me. Something with a shirt and tie. Or maybe even a clerical collar. But we rolled on."

The Mikkelsens left Highway 61 on Snelling Avenue in Saint Paul, went past the State Fairgrounds, and on to the campus. And there, parked in front of the fieldhouse just as he'd told Vern he would be, was Al Holst.

The man whose flat tire altered the course of history for Mikkelsen was to help him make another decision—where to live as the summer was giving way to autumn.

"As Dad drove away, heading home, Al pointed to the passenger seat in the Buick and said, 'Get in.' And I did. Then I got a little nervous. I saw the classified section of a *Saint Paul Pioneer Press* between us with what appeared to be several pencil circles around rentals.

"I wondered what this was all about. Was he shipping me off to somewhere? It seems he had one place in mind for me as we went down south on Snelling past Marshall Avenue. We finally stopped a half block off Snelling. But it was right across the street from Macalester College. I didn't understand why. But that was to be my home till the end of my first year. It seemed strange to me—going to Hamline but living right by Macalester.

"That fall, I saw more 'Mac' kids than Hamline kids. But Al, who had known exactly when Dad and I would drive up to Hamline that day, knew it would work for me, and it did." Separated from the social aspect of college, Mikkelsen attended class and became accustomed to fitting in times to study. He also got well acquainted with the fieldhouse basketball court.

But there was a spot of trouble ahead. Vern recalls, "After about three weeks of classes, I got a call from Dad. Now you must realize that I was well aware of how urgent this must be. People just did not call long distance on a whim in those days. It was too expensive.

"I thought I could sense some dissatisfaction in my dad's voice. He told me that he had received a letter from the Hamline financial office—Harold Craig. Dad said he had been asked for the money to cover my enrollment. He simply had very little money, so this made him terribly unhappy, and that is probably an understatement. Dad believed this had all been settled earlier.

"He told me to stay right there at the fieldhouse where I had been called to the telephone and that he would be right down. And down from Askov he came, getting a bit hotter all the way. I got hold of Al Holst and told him that my dad was upset because of the message he had received from the business office.

"Holst met with my dad at the fieldhouse and told Dad that he, too, thought everything had been taken care of, but that Dad would have to meet with Charles Nelson Pace, no less than president of the university. My dad asked Al where this Mr. Pace might be found. Al told Dad that it was a Saturday morning and that President Pace would be watching football practice.

"I could see my dad fuming and muttering something to himself about 'this Methodist place' under his breath, but he said, 'Let's go.' And off the three of us went. I was not real happy with this development, as you can imagine. First, everything had been going so nicely with classes and all. No hitch that I had noticed. And everyone knows that kids don't like to be around close when their father is raising hell. I stayed as much as I could in the background.

"Holst introduced my dad to President Pace and then stepped away as the two of them talked. The situation was discussed quickly and in a friendly way, for which I was thankful. Then the president said to my dad that if that is what Holst promised, then it was agreed upon and that's all there was to it. Holst seemed as relieved as I was. President Pace apologized to my dad about the misunderstanding, then returned to watching football as my dad hustled back to Askov to prepare for Sunday services.

"The next four years, there was never a question. My tuition was all paid."

Holst had intervened in Vern's life at a time when Vern felt that he was bound, like so many Minnesota kids, then and now, to attend a public college or university. "Holst testified to Hamline that I was a good prospect, in basketball and in academics, even though it was more good faith than anything. He'd never seen me play. Al helped me think about the fact that if I went to the U I would be competing for playing time with Jim McIntyre, who had just led Minneapolis Henry to two straight state championships. He was bigger, older—remember I had just turned sixteen in October of 1944—and more experienced at what I figured was big-time competition. They thought I might get lost in the shuffle at the 'U'. Al was especially convincing.

"It was Al who also explained to me that Hamline's star center, Howie Schultz, had graduated but was sticking around to help coach, the newcomers mostly, for Coach Joe Hutton. It was Al, finally, who helped me understand that the best thing for me was to be a Piper. And it turned out that it sure was."

Mikkelsen's relationship with Holst remained extremely warm through the years, and it came to a close only with Holst's untimely death in 1964.

That year Vern was invited to play in a special old-timers' all-star game as part of the festivities associated within the

The Old-Timer's game: Boston, 1965
Back row: Arnie Johnson, Jim Pollard, Jack Coleman, Arnie Risen, George
Mikan, Vern Mikkelsen. Front Row: Max Zaslofsky, Les Harrison (coach),
Bob Davies, Bobby Wanzer, Al Cervi, Slater Martin

NBA All-Star game being held in Boston. On the West team with Mikkelsen were Arnie Johnson, Jim Pollard, Jack Coleman, Arnie Risen, George Mikan, Max Zaslofsky, Coach Les Harrison, Bob Davies, Bobby Wanzer, Al Cervi, and Slater Martin. As Vern was kicking up his heels with his somewhat elderly pals on the Boston Garden court, Al Holst was watching the game on television at his home in Buffalo, Minnesota, where he had been superintendent of schools. In a sad conclusion to an enduring friendship, Holst, who had been having heart difficulties, died while watching the game.

Upon Vern's return to Minneapolis from Boston two days later, he learned from his wife Jean of Al's death. He rushed to the funeral being held that very afternoon in Buffalo.

"I hurried to the church," Vern recalls. "I arrived at the church just as the service was starting. I sat in the back of the church, trying to be respectful yet out of the way. An attendant spotted me and came to the back pew to ask me to come up front to the casket—which already had been closed—to pay my last respects to Al.

"I did that; the casket was re-opened. That took a few minutes. I stood there with these mixed feelings, my fondness for Al and yet my embarrassment at the trouble I was causing. However, it was worth it. I got to spend a last few moments with Al, thinking of our shared history, before returning to my seat for the rest of the service. At a reception afterward, I spent time with Al's family. I was told he had said before the game how pleased he would be to see me play one last time, meaning that it would probably be the last time I'd play a meaningful game. And that was it."

4

The Piper is an All-Star

The scholarship bestowed on the small town kid from Askov came from a school with a rich history in both academics and athletics. Hamline University was founded in 1854 in Red Wing, Minnesota, as the first institution of higher education in the state. (The University of Minnesota is technically older, having been chartered in 1851, but it did not begin enrolling students until 1857.) Fitting too for the Mikkelsen story, Hamline was the birthplace of inter-collegiate basketball. James Naismith invented the game in 1891, and Ray Kaighn, who later became Hamline's Athletic Director, played on Naismith's very first basketball team. Kaighn brought the sport to the University in 1893, when it was barely a year old. He organized a women's program two years later, and on February 9, 1895, Hamline hosted the first intercollegiate basketball game in history, succumbing to the Minnesota State School of Agriculture (which later became the St. Paul Campus of the University of Minnesota) by a score of 9 to 3. The game was played in the basement of the school's old science building (now long since demol-ished) and featured nine players to a side.

By the time Vern arrived on campus in late summer of 1945, the game had evolved considerably, and Hamline, its modest enrollment notwithstanding, had developed an enviable reputation as a basketball powerhouse under Coach Joe Hutton.

Vern's arrival on campus made an impression on Keith Paisley, a classmate and friend who later became a South Dakota State Senator. "In the late summer of 1945," Paisley recently recalled, "an awkward and seemingly art- less 16-year-old country boy emerged upon the campus of Hamline University. Verner Mikkelsen, at nearly six-foot-five

Hutton & Schultz

inches, had badly out- grown his clothes and his high school back- ground at tiny Askov, the rutabaga capitol of Minnesota. He gave little evidence that he could possibly be a worthy heir to his pre- decessor at the center position, the urbane Howie Schultz.

He had a series of campus jobs at per- haps fifty cents an hour, including the garbage detail at the men's dormitory and dining hall. Vern liked this just fine. He set out to prove he really could be unyielding both on and off the basket- ball court. He committed himself to the academic regimen and humbly to the very normal flow of campus life which included joining the choir. He was quietly tenacious, unas- suming, and willing to pledge himself to this new life which he had found."

Vern's freshman season

When Vern arrived Coach Hutton was in Europe with other coaches of note keeping spirits high for Americans returning from service duty in the closing days of World War II, and Howie Schultz was given the assignment of welcoming the young Dane to Hamline basketball. It was an interesting challenge for Schultz, who had helped the school to its 1942 national small-college basketball championship and later played both basketball and baseball professionally at the major-league level.

The "teacher" and the "student" worked together daily in the same manner that, a year or two earlier, Coach Ray Meyer had tutored George Mikan in the paths to success around and under a basketball net at DePaul.

Mikkelsen says, "Howie Schultz turned me from a guy who played basketball into a basketball player."

"And what a kid he was," Schultz later recalled. "Liquid

[receptive] wrists. With good talent. And a bright kid, too. What he learned, he didn't forget."

The first personal challenge Mikkelsen faced at Hamline was to move ahead of the center that the school had recruited in more standard fashion, 6-foot-7 fellow-freshman Johnny Haefner of Stillwater. In no time at all, Mikkelsen stood alone in the center position.

But it was endless hours with the 6-foot-6 Schultz that earned "most improved" citations for the Askov product day after day after day. During those special drills with Schultz in his first year, Vern had grown to 6-foot-5 and weighed 185 pounds. The kid from the sticks was beginning to look less like a stick himself and more like a basketball man. Before long Mik (as his friends had begun to call him) moved into a sleeping room in the fieldhouse with teammate and classmate Bob "Fish" Leiviska of Virginia, Minnesota, who would become one of his closest friends and business associates over the next thirty years.

Mikkelsen remembers fondly those first weeks at Hamline.

Vern as a freshman

"Although I still had not met Coach Hutton, Howie worked me hard—after regular practice, after scrimmages, any time I wanted to work. I had so much admiration for him, a championship-team basketball player at the school in 1942 and a first baseman for the Brooklyn Dodgers, who had been eliminated that 1945 season in the National League race. He had me do things over and over around the basket until he was assured I knew what I was doing. There's no way to describe how much it helped me. I just turned seventeen that October, and for the first time I felt comfortable with things as they happened on the court.

"I can't forget my first meeting with Coach Hutton when he returned from Europe. The first question he asked me was, 'How did you end up with three science subjects?' He said that with five late-afternoon classes in physics, chemistry, and geology, I wouldn't have time to practice.

"He had me change my major to physical education, but I was still able to work in tough subjects. And some music participation, too. Howie continued to work with me after practices, but I still was pretty raw when we went into Chicago for a four-team Christmas tournament. Growing fast, I was closing in on 6-foot-5½ and had gotten near 200 pounds. But the other guys who were to be playing in the middle in that Chicago Stadium tournament were huge. There was Mikan at 6-10 for DePaul, Don Otten of Bowling Green at 6-11, and Bob Kurland of Oklahoma A&M at seven feet, all of them quite experienced, of course, compared to me."

It was, in the truest sense, a baptism of fire for Schultz's protégé. What his personal coach had referred to as liquid wrists approximated what others might term (in baseball and football) as soft hands. Mikkelsen, in a natural way that was refined during the hours of work with Schultz, would cradle the most crisp of passes from his teammates in his welcoming hands. And, in much the same fashion, he was able to get up soft shots out of the crashing melee that often resulted from the warfare under the backboard. A future was being formed.

Howie Schlutz

The entry of Schultz into Mikkelsen's life was as dramatic as the remarkable intrusion two years earlier of Al Holst.

Schultz was a product of juvenile sports in St. Paul. He

had helped Hamline to its 1942 small-college basketball championship and had also played high-level professional baseball. At that time the National Association of Intercollegiate Athletics, previously called the National Association of Intercollegiate Basketball, allowed an athlete to play professionally in one sport while retaining collegiate eligibility in others, so Schultz had been able to play for the Dodgers as well as their farm club, the St. Paul Saints, and still compete at Hamline in basketball. Schultz played baseball with Philadelphia and Cincinnati

Mik playing against Mikan, 1945

after his stint the Dodgers, but he retired from baseball after the 1948 season. Jackie Robinson had come along at his position. He also played pro basketball for six years—three in the National Basketball League and three in the NBA. In 1946-47 he started playing for the Packers of Anderson, Indiana, then became a player-coach there for three more seasons, including 1949-50, when the franchise had been part of the new NBA.

During the closing days of that season, Schultz signed on for a short stint with the Fort Wayne, Indiana, Zollner Pistons. In 1951-52 he joined the Lakers, along with fellow Hamline graduate Joey Hutton, and averaged four points a game playing front-line relief for Mikan, Mikkelsen, and Pollard.

But all of that was yet to come. In 1945 Mikkelsen was the aspiring student and Schultz was the seasoned pro who had drawn the assignment of fine-tuning the raw but eager Dane from Askov. That eagerness was tested when the Pipers traveled to Chicago for the Christmas tournament. Mikkelsen recalls, "I was still a pretty crude freshman when we went into Chicago Stadium for that competition. Yes, Howie did things with me that Coach Meyer had done earlier with Mikan. But now I was to meet The Man himself on the court. In front of thousands of people. If I wasn't scared—and I don't remember that I was—then it was just because I was too numb to be scared.

"Rollie Seltz [another Piper who went on to professional basketball, four years of it with Anderson and Waterloo] was a senior forward then and our only real tested player. We got beat handily by DePaul, as some 21,000 watched. I remember I got a basket off George early and actually apologized. He said, 'That's OK kid, you won't get any more.' And I don't think that I did. It was a scary start for my basketball career." But others, such as Schultz and Seltz, saw only the infinite possibilities. Coach Hutton had been in Europe on his USO assignment when the Chicago tournament possibility presented itself. Mikkelsen recalls that Hutton's first wife, Janet, actually signed the contract on behalf of her traveling husband to finalize the Pipers' 1945-46 schedule.

One newspaper account of the Chicago adventure related that "the Chicago fans gave 'Mik' a fine ovation when they learned that he was only seventeen years old, but willing to go to work on Mikan and Otten, a pair of All-Americans with years of experience." And Hutton called the Askov export "most improved player on our squad." Whoever might have been making the assessment, they were part of a consensus opinion that Hamline had a marvelous post player in the making. The ripening prospect had grown in many ways since his days as a 5-foot-10 ninth-grader in Pine County.

Another thought about Mikkelsen was expressed by Ken Thompson, Vern's teammate his first two seasons with the Pipers. Thompson had played some as a freshman on the Pipers' 1942 championship team. Following a two-year stint in the Navy, he returned to Hamline to complete his education. "I saw that the new kid, Vern, a freshman, was big, strong, and somewhat awkward, but more than willing to do whatever work was necessary to improve. The weekend that we played in the Chicago Stadium, he held his own pretty well with Mikan of DePaul and Don Otten.

"Coach Joe Hutton saw Vern continue to gain confidence against the many big-college teams on our schedule," Thompson continued. "And with the addition of Hal Haskins, they added another national [small-college] championship trophy to Hamline's display case in 1949. Vern made four trips to Kansas City for the NAIA tournament.

My senior year, I was captain and we had a 22-5 record, losing I believe to Marshall in the second round at Kansas City. We had a 'best win' that season over Stanford. I felt like I could be Vern's older brother. I was nine years older. He participated in track and field, which helped his agility and jumping ability. He was rugged on the backboards and had extremely sharp elbows."

Thompson spent his after-college life in athletic coaching and administration at Worthington High School in southwestern Minnesota. Of his own Piper experience, Thompson said, "During the 1940s and 1950s in the Twin Cities, Hamline basketball was the best show in town, playing to full houses each night.

"The popularity was due to the gentleman doing the coaching, MISTER Hutton. With no full-time assistant [though Schultz and Harold Montgomery helped], the accomplishment was his alone. I feel privileged to have been a part, with teammates early on such as John Norlander and Howie Schultz, and after the [Navy] service with stars such as Vern and Hal Haskins, who helped win the national tournament two years after I graduated. Winning was so much fun." Like so many of the Hamline athletes, including Seltz and, of course, Schultz, Thompson was an excellent baseball player in amateur ranks.

In addition to the Marshall second-round loss in the 1947 NAIA tournament in Kansas City, Mikkelsen and the Pipers fell to Louisville once and to an Indiana State team coached by John Wooden a year before he went west to coach at UCLA. The Marshall loss was 55-54 and the Pipers were close in the other two NAIA tourney losses as well, all of which were to schools that now sport Division 1 NCAA teams. In 1949, when Vern was a senior, the Pipers won the NAIA national championship.

All the while, Hamline was defeating with unchanging regularity its Minnesota Intercollegiate Athletic Conference rivals such as St. Olaf, Gustavus, Macalester, Augsburg, St. Thomas, St. John's, Concordia of Moorhead, and St. Mary's of Winona. The 1948-49 season included lop-sided victories over other regional foes such as North Dakota State, the University of North Dakota, and River Falls, Wisconsin. MIAC foe St. Thomas, beaten earlier by the Pipers, notched a 45-43 win over Hamline a few weeks before the team's only other two losses in a national-title season. The losses were to the Amateur Athletic Union powerhouse Phillips 66ers, who defeated them 52-38 and 49-46 in exhibition games in the Twin Cities.

During that unforgettable season, with Harold Montgomery assisting Coach Hutton, the most important number for Hamline was the big 13 on Mikkelsen's jersey. Never was that more evident than on New Year's Eve. As 1948 gave way to 1949, Mik, now a solid 6-foot-7 and 225 pounds, though still only twenty years old, was named most-valuable player of the Los Angeles Invitational, as the Pipers turned back Los Angeles Loyola 54-40, Wyoming 37-35, and Pepperdine 62-38 in the championship game on New Year's Eve. That title march capped an arduous Christmas-time journey that had begun with a dedication tournament for a new Denver Fieldhouse. In that one, the Pipers defeated Denver University (with Vince Boryla, later a New York Knick opponent of Vern) 60-54 and Texas Christian 66-47.

From Denver the Huttonmen traveled on December 23 to San Francisco for a Cow Palace victory over Santa

The Hamline team heads west, 1948

Clara 60-53. In all, the celebration of a Colorado/California Christmas was intoxicating stuff for ten bold Upper Midwest athletes enjoying the ride of their lives.

In addition to the wins listed above, the Pipers had a 70-35 season-opening win over Valparaiso and another 60-42 conquest of the Indiana-based Crusaders at midseason. In all, the team won thirty games that season against three losses, two of them considered exhibitions against the powerful Phillips aggregation.

At Kansas City, Hamline became the first school to win the NAIB title twice. The Pipers were the most highly regarded of all 1949 entrants because of their accomplishments against NCAA major colleges. Late in the regular season, following losses by the University of Minnesota, Western Kentucky, and Villanova, a newspaper picture of Mikkelsen, Joey Hutton, Duane Meyer, Haskins, and Leiviska carried the comment:

The last major undefeated college team, 1949.
Left to right: Duane Meyer, Bob "Fish" Leiviska, Hal Haskins,
Vern Mikkelsen, Joe Hutton, Jr.

"the last major undefeated quint." Minnesota's season, of course, was buoyed by the performance of Jim McIntyre, who was breaking all the Big Ten Conference scoring records and making some All-America teams.

To win their NAIB crown, the 1949 Pipers, over the space of six days, defeated Arkansas State 76-43, Indiana Central 83-66, Texas Tech 80-53, Beloit, Wisconsin, 52-43 and Regis of Denver 57-46 as crowds of up to eight thousand watched nightly in Kansas City's Municipal Auditorium.

Haskins and Mikkelsen were named co-captains of the NAIB All-America team, and Haskins was picked as the tournament's most-valuable player after scoring 103 points in the five games. Mikkelsen himself contributed 92 points. Among the perks the title gave Hamline was a trip to Honolulu the following season, hosted by the University of Hawaii. Mikkelsen, Meyer, and Leiviska, who had a hand in the momentous previous season as seniors, could only wish the underclassmen a year-early bon voyage for the 1949-50 season.

Dozing some, and dreaming, too, on the Rock Island Rocket headed back to St. Paul from Kansas City after the tournament, Mik says he reflected "on how tremendous our Hamline fans had been. There were some six-hundred of them who had traveled by bus to Kansas City. They held roaring pep rallies on the streets near the Kansas City Auditorium. I thought back to specific games, like a few early in my career, when the Great Lakes Navy team came to our campus to play us. They were older guys who taught us a few things. Then there was a game against American International in the Boston Garden when the center job was finally all mine, and a game against Valparaiso when I realized I could play with guys as big as their 6-foot-9 Milt Schoon. Kenny Merritt and Seltz had big games as we slipped past them 34-32. I began to see why Coach Hutton always placed so much emphasis on rebounding and defense." Mikkelsen's best game may have been against Texas Tech late in his senior season, when he scored thirteen field goals in sixteen shots in an 80-53 victory.

The clicking of train wheels on rails also reminded Mik somehow of the first time the Pipers traveled by air to a game at Fargo to play Concordia-Moorhead only two months earlier. "We thought we were pretty classy then," he said.

For the rest of the Pipers, the trip home from Kansas City was a salute to a successful season completed.

Not so with Mikkelsen.

He was selected to play in the prestigious East-West College All-Star Basketball Game later that spring—the first small-college player ever to receive that honor. The game was held on April 2, 1949, in New York's Madison Square Garden for the benefit of the *New York Herald Tribune* Fresh Air Fund.

He would go up against an East squad coached by Adolph Rupp, legendary coach who had been in Europe in the fall of 1945 with Joe Hutton. On Rupp's team were four of his Kentucky All-Americans, Alex Groza, Ralph Beard, Wah Wah Jones, and Cliff Barker. Others to play for East were Yale's Tony Lavelli, leading scorer till then in major-college basketball history; Ed Leede, Dartmouth; Dick McGuire, St. John's of New York; Warren Perkins, Tulane; Frank  "Pep" Saul, Seton Hall (from 1951 to 1954 to be Mik's Laker teammate); and Ernie Vandeweghe of Colgate. In both 1948 and 1949, Kentucky won national Division 1 championships and Groza was picked as Player of the Year.

At 6-foot-7, Groza understandably was the player most in Mikkelsen's thoughts as he looked forward to the game. He admits it was difficult to concentrate. "We had a full week in New York at the famous Lexington Hotel. I was kind of unsung as the only small-school guy there, but Coach Vadal Peterson of Utah assured me I'd spend time in the post against Groza along with Easy Ed Macauley, a two-year All-America center from St. Louis University.

"By another of those strange coincidences that kept popping up in my life, my two West-team roommates were Slater "Dugie" Martin of Texas and Bob Harrison of Michigan. Both Dugie and Harrison were to be drafted by the Lakers as I would be. "

Others on the West squad were Vern Gardner, Utah; Bill Evans, Drake; Paul Courty, Oklahoma; Cliff Crandall, Oregon State; Leon Barnhorst, Notre Dame; and John Parks, Oklahoma A&M. Macauley and Gardner, as All-Americans, were the West's headliners for the game, which found the East heavily favored.

As had been the case all of his competitive life, Mikkelsen had a big surprise in store for the big-school boys and the crowds that had worshipped them. Roger Rosenblum's account in the *St. Paul Pioneer Press* told the story: "A jam-packed Madison Square Garden crowd of 18,341 watched as a hand-picked team of Eastern All-Stars shaded the West 65-64 despite the efforts of Hamline's Vern Mikkelsen. Mikkelsen not only scored 17 points to top all performers, but provided the spark needed to keep the West within striking distance.

"West coach Peterson expressed disappointment when Mikkelsen did not receive the most-valuable player award [won by] Groza. Peterson said, 'I think Mikkelsen's performance spoke for itself.' Beard scored 13 points, Groza 12 and Jones 11 for the East, which trailed at the half 37-35. Barnhorst was the only other double-figure scorer for the West with 11."

So Vern's All-Star collegiate basketball odyssey came to an end in a place where no rutabaga would grow—Madison Square Garden. New Yorkers were added to the growing list of Mikkelsen fans!

Where next, Super Dane?

Vern greets his parents after returning home from the All-Star Game, 1949

5

Phillips 66ers or Lakers?

Verner Mikkelsen was contemplating his future, as he had done many times before. Would it be in music or athletics? Then, one snowy day in February of 1949, Cab Renick came to town.

Renick, the coach, chief architect, and strong recruiting agent for the globetrotting Phillips 66ers, the crack semi-professional basketball team from Bartlesville, Oklahoma, had Mikkelsen under close scrutiny when the Hamline University senior least expected it. The Pipers were dissecting St. Olaf in basketball one night as anticipated, winning 50-34 with Renick in the stands. Accompanying the 66ers' boss was his star player, Bob Kurland. This was the same Kurland who had seen Mikkelsen as a freshman three years earlier, when Vern and Joe Hutton's ambitious Hamline squad invaded Chicago Stadium.

As St. Olaf fell, Mik scored twenty points in twenty minutes in a brief but impressive showing that Renick understood full well. He had been following Mikkelsen's career with particular interest. That week his 66ers were to take on Hamline in a pair of exhibition games in the Twin Cities for charity. More to the point, the visit would provide Renick with an opportunity to explain to Vern the beauty of Amateur Athletic Union basketball—of which his 66ers were a prime example.

In the next two nights, 11,000 spectators would watch the small-college Pipers take on the cream of "independent" basketball—3,000 in Hamline's Norton Fieldhouse and 8,000 the following night in the Minneapolis Auditorium.

At the time, Hamline was ranked ninth nationally among all college teams, from big or small schools (the Pipers being the only "small" school so represented). The 66ers had a 41-3 record headed into the unusual doubleheader, which was primarily a benefit for the local Sister Kenny Polio Fund, though a group of Hamline backers was also planning to use a portion of the proceeds to purchase a gift for Hamline's venerable coach, Joe Hutton. What was acknowledged as the nation's best "amateur" team won 52-38 on Hamline's court. Mikkelsen accounted for 16 of the Pipers' points (the hosts later lamenting their despicable shooting—12 field goals in 69 shots). Kurland had 12 points before fouling out with three minutes remaining. The next evening in Minneapolis, the 66ers, with Kurland not much of a factor, hung on to win 49-46 as Mikkelsen scored 18 points and versatile teammate Hal Haskins had 16. Renick called Hamline "the best college team we have played." Coach Hutton received a new Mercury in honor of his solid coaching history at Hamline, and the Sister Kenny Fund also received its expected share of the gate.

Mikkelsen's two impressive games against Kurland, the 66ers 7-foot center, prompted Renick to continue his coaxing of Mik to join the Phillips Petroleum Company and its nomadic basketball team.

It was revealed in later years that the less-than-capacity second-night crowd caused the "H Club" of Hamline backers to make up the money difference on the car. Hutton said, "I thought I was going to be presented with a scrapbook of the team. I walked right by the car on the way to the floor for the second half, but I didn't pay any attention to it. Boy, was I surprised by the wonderful gift."

Until those two nights against the 66ers, Mikkelsen had remained uncertain about his post-graduation way of life. He had been advised that the Lakers also were monitoring his progress carefully. Where would the Askov native venture from here?

Renick's zealous overtures did not have the result the 66ers' skipper desired, but they did convince the Hamline senior that basketball—the professional brand—would dominate the coming years, if he could raise his game to that level of expertise. The 66ers' persistence seemed to assure him that he could. The music? The teaching? Perhaps the high school coaching? All would be set aside for the present.

A Career in Music?

"The more basketball I played in college, the more passion I had for it," Mik said. "On the other hand, in many ways I liked music even more—and it wasn't all just the pretty girls in the choir."

Though Mik continued to explore the possibility of a future teaching school, perhaps in music, and even doing some coaching, his inquiries led him eventually to relegate that career-choice to the "back-burner."

Yet a dozen years earlier things had not been not so simple. For the youngster Verner Mikkelsen, music won out easily over athletics for the Number One spot in his head and heart. In fact, it was no contest. He as yet did not know what a basketball was, or anything else to do with sports—except gymnastics, a Danish favorite.

Music was winning his affection by "a country mile," as Vern would say later. And that is how far Vern would walk on Sunday mornings to the Danish Lutheran Church his father

Vern as a freshman in the Hamline
A Capella Choir

tended in northeast Montana, listening all the way to the organ's sounds piercing the dry, dusty air as he approached.

"Much of my interest in music was fostered by my mother," Vern said. "She was an excellent piano and organ player. She was church organist whenever my father needed her to do that.

"I can remember vividly Saturdays in the parsonage [whether an older home such as in Wisconsin or a newer one as in Montana]. My dad would have the list of hymns to be sung on Sunday. Mom would play them on the piano and she and my dad would sing them." In time, Vern would learn to join in at those special weekly occasions.

When the family lived in Askov, Vern would join Byron Petersen and two girls in a quartet that would sing a hymn after Pastor Mikkelsen left the pulpit to give general messages and announcements. So, in church as well as school, where he played saxophone and snare drums, music was a companion.

It was not surprising, therefore, that while attending Hamline, Mikkelsen yearned to sing in the school's a cappella choir, directed by Bob Holliday. "It was a very prestigious choir," Vern said. "All of the voices were music majors. I asked if I could try out for it. I was told that I could, but only because they were short of male voices due to men still in the service awaiting discharge after World War II. I was completely shocked to make it.

"I sang for three years, then had to quit because there was too much of a conflict my senior year with basketball.

"Maybe when I quit it was an indication that I knew where my future lay; but in many, many ways I enjoyed choir more than basketball. The choir made great road trips, just like basketball. Many places we sang were just plain fun.

"One in particular was a trip Holliday had arranged for a concert at a Rotary Club luncheon at the St. Paul Athletic Club. We were to do two numbers following the luncheon. We filed in in single-file and took our places on the risers. I was the last one up on the podium, by far the tallest person in the room. Now, the Rotarians were not ashamed to have a couple of bumps before lunch, so you can imagine the place was a little rambunctious by the time we were to sing. Because of my height, I could hear a few comments as I brought up the rear. When I got to the top riser with the rest of the bass voices, I stood up straight and cracked my head on the ceiling. Many of the Rotarians knew who I was and smiled when that happened. Holliday very quietly motioned me down to the next row, but it was no better—cramped quarters.

"Finally, I was down with the altos. The Rotarians did their best not to notice, but some of them couldn't resist commenting to one another.

"Away from the rest of the group after we sang, Holliday suggested I would have to make a decision. Either hoops or choir. We agreed at the end of my junior year it would be time for me to leave. It was difficult for me because I so enjoyed singing a cappella. Yes, in many ways more than basketball. As I look back, maybe it was the girls."

Mikkelsen was one of the few athletes that got to be in the choir. "Mr. Holliday used to say to me," he later recalled, "'Well, I suppose you have to go off to basketball rehearsal now.' He called our practice 'rehearsal.' He was quite a guy."

A high spot for Mikkelsen in the Hamline A Cappella choir came when it was rehearsing a very difficult presentation of Bach's "Come Jesus Come." It was to be done with the choir split in two. "It was very difficult, particularly for me because I was not a music major. We worked on the presentation for several weeks. Finally, the day of reckoning came for me. Four of us in each of the two choirs had to sing our presentation solo. There was a soprano, alto, tenor, and bass—me. The eight finished our oratorios [dramatic text]. Choir members surprised me with a standing ovation. They were proud of me because they knew I was a long shot to complete the "Come Jesus Come"—you can't imagine how difficult this solo was for me. I felt real good, finishing the presentation."

In addition to basketball and choir, Mikkelsen was a member of the all-college council, president of the junior class, and president of the Lutheran Students Association. He also participated in track and was on the health council. He would have been involved in drama also, if he'd had the time.

While Vern was attending Hamline, his parents moved to Minneapolis after spending seven years at Askov. Among the accomplishments of their son, they were proud that he was a member of a singing quartet which made appearances around the Twin Cities. With all of that, Mikkelsen was better than a "B" student in the classroom.

Perhaps the most astute basketball-related comment regarding this remarkable athlete, who had by this time reached 6-foot-7, was attributed to Coach Hutton, who said, "He's still learning, shouldn't reach his peak until after he has left Hamline." Not yet twenty-one, Mik graduated in four years, then turned his full attention to a future in basketball.

Many were the hours that Mikkelsen toiled in various jobs on campus, contributing his time in exchange for an education. Some may have thought he would earn a master-of-the-mower degree for all the time spent leveling Hamline's grass in spring and early autumn. While pushing the mower, Vern could be excused if his mind was balancing the regional trips made with the choir (and those beautiful sopranos and altos) against basketball journeys like the one to the West Coast that found the Pipers marooned for a time in Wyoming when a few passenger trains were halted by a severe winter blizzard.

The choir traveled to South America once to give concerts, but the long basketball season, which stretched from early fall practices to late-winter tournaments, prevented Vern from going.

Wherever Vern went, he had one constant companion, the well-worn Bible his parents presented him when he was

Hal Haskins (l), Vern (c), and Bob "Fish" Leiviska (r) at camp

confirmed in the Danish Lutheran Church. In Danish, May 17, 1942, was known to Vern and his mom and dad as kon-fermations-dagen. "The Bible has always been a good friend of mine," he said.

He worked three summers in high school at the (Art) Otis Lodge near Grand Rapids, Minnesota. "The lodge was unusual in that Grand Rapids had a small airport out toward the Otis property," he said. "Many guests flew in, and I washed planes and generally mowed grass and cleaned things up at the airport. It was then I first became fascinated with airplanes, a feeling I had until my legs got so long I had problems sitting in them."

But now, graduation day loomed.

"By the day I graduated from Hamline," Mikkelsen said, "I was pretty well set that I would give the Lakers a try. I was more confident with my game every day of my senior year. The Phillips people had boosted my confidence with their interest in me. And I was beginning to read things written by people I respected that said I could help this world championship team, which already had the greatest center around in George Mikan. In fact, it was Mikan's presence that troubled me. How in the world was I going to get to play with him at my position?"

Dick Cullum, a leading Twin Cities sports columnist of his day, wrote at the time: "It appears to be well settled that the Minneapolis Lakers have decided upon Vern Mikkelsen of Hamline as the man they want to understudy George Mikan next season, even in preference to All-American Jim McIntyre [University of Minnesota].

"Each team [in the NBA may] designate one player in its home territory who will not go into the general draft but may be negotiated with by the home team only. The Lakers—above everything—need someone who can play Mikan's position while George catches his breath.

"George has played nearly every minute of every game this [1948-49] season. He has displayed amazing stamina. Although there are two or three men on him much of the time, all giving him every bump and nudge they can get away with, he remains the outstanding player of the league. But he is pretty well used up now [for the season]. Moreover, he is much too valuable a piece of property to be subjected to such strain that he may lose his full effectiveness before his time."

The problem described by Cullum was to be solved, but in a way neither Cullum nor anyone else could foresee at the time.

Cullum continued, "What good fortune, then, that two of the best college centers in the country are residents of the Twin Cities. The Lakers may take their choice and no other league team may enter a competitive bid. Mikkelsen is so good that the Lakers prefer him. The Lakers say he appears to be better suited for the professional game where stamina is a chief factor. The Lakers are convinced he will do well in professional basketball. They are convinced, to be more specific about it, that he is just the man to give Mikan the help he needs."

Cullum was writing immediately after Hamline won the 1949 small-college championship at Kansas City—at exactly the time that Mikkelsen was wondering just a bit about what kind of basketball was in his future.

Music Man indeed. But what type of "court music" would he be orchestrating in the years to come?

Mikkelsen also was pondering the recent games against the Phillips 66ers, during which he had competed against seasoned players from Coach Renick's squad. He could not help but notice that in order to pull away successfully in the second game of the two-night series, the 66ers coach (who preferred "Cab" to his given name of Jesse) began to ignore Kurland, the man Mikkelsen was defending, and look elsewhere on the court for points. Mikkelsen took this as another indication that he was a basketball player of considerable promise on both ends of the court.

In addition to pondering whether he had the ability, Mikkelsen also had to consider whether he could *afford* to play. The NBA was at that time in its infancy as a successor to the Basketball Association of America, and incoming players were not automatically showered with riches.

Among the players of Vern's 1949 draft class, Dick McGuire, Al's brother and the territorial pick by the Knicks out of St. John's (NY), expressed doubts about even being able to make a living at basketball. Though he was a success, McGuire was often quoted later in life as saying, "I couldn't believe it."

To Mikkelsen, however, who was twenty, single, and not in a hurry to look for a wife, the financial end seemed rather unimportant. "I just wanted to prove to myself that I could do it," he said. That he would have funds to rent an apartment and later to purchase a home in South Minneapolis, near Minnehaha Falls (to return to the lawn mowing of his youth, you know), were about all that Mikkelsen really required in terms of cash in those days.

Yet Mik's love of music remained a dogged presence in his life, stubbornly refusing to be set aside. During the summer between his junior and senior years at Hamline, and also during the months after graduation, Mikkelsen joined Bob "Fish" Leiviska and "Sleepy Hal" Haskins on the staff of a boys camp on Lake Pokegama southwest of Grand Rapids. "We worked with a bunch of Carleton kids as cabin leaders and directors of various activities." This work brought Vern exquisitely back into contact with the realm of music. He worked with campers who had special interests along those lines. He concluded his boys camp duties playing the lead in a cast of campers in the Gilbert and Sullivan operetta *The Pirates of Penzance* ... one king-sized seaman.

Later, with the Lakers, his love of music stayed with him in fascinating ways. When standing next to each other during the "The Star Spangled Banner" before games, he and all-pro Jim Pollard would harmonize. They took turns singing lead and harmony, then critiquing each other's work. During the 1950-51 season Mikkelsen formed a quartet with Pollard, former Minneapolis Edison and University of Minnesota athlete Tony Jaros, and Irish tenor Kevin O'Shea, out of Notre Dame. Were they in great demand to perform? Perhaps, but doubtful.

Tony Jarus, Jim Pollard, Kevin O'Shea, and Vern

But that is getting ahead of the story. What of the Great Dane's momentous career decision during the summer of '49? "I had seen what I could do against an awful lot of heralded college players during regular-season games at Hamline. And the 66ers stars came from Oklahoma State, Oregon State, Arkansas, UCLA, and Oklahoma. The East-West game demonstrated favorably to me that I could—I hope this doesn't sound cocky—hold my own pretty much anywhere with college players. But I realized only the very best made it in the pros so I remained apprehensive."

From the New York experience against the Eastern Stars, two West teammates, Slater Martin and Bob Harrison, were to join Mik as Laker draftees. "That made me a bit more comfortable," he said.

If he joined the Lakers, he would be exposed to a different coaching style—the soft-spoken ways of John Kundla. He did not fear the switch. "I knew of Kundla's tremendous success. Yet in my mind, Joe Hutton was one of the top five or six coaches in the country. He had the total respect of his ball players, exactly what I heard that Kundla had."

Finally, Vern could not resist comparing his situation as a college graduate with his thoughts coming out of high school four years earlier. Minnesota's Gophers had shown considerable interest. But Hamline's Al Holst had placed his foot squarely in the family's Askov door. Vern had made a choice, albeit a difficult one. Hamline rather than the "U". And it had worked out superbly.

"People whose opinions I respected had advised me not to go to Minnesota because I would get lost in the shuffle," Mikkelsen said. "And Hamline seemed to need me more because Howie Schultz had graduated out of the center position and now was freshman coach." So he became a Piper rather than a Gopher. It appeared increasingly likely that he would be trading Hamline Red and Gray for Minneapolis Laker Blue and Gold (colors taken from the Swedish flag for some undisclosed reason).

6

Along Came Mikan

It would be inaccurate to state that Vern Mikkelsen knew all along that he would one day be a Minneapolis Laker. Rather, the realization came to him by degrees.

The first positive qualifying aspect would be the realization, after the first few months at Hamline University, that he could play pretty good basketball. He enjoyed the physical part of crashing bodies.

Second, the personal coaching he received from Howie Schultz and the game philosophy he was presented by Coach Joe Hutton were in Vern's eyes unequaled at the college level.

Third, during his senior year there was the small-college championship, and, of perhaps even greater importance, routine success against major-college opposition. The accolades that he, forwards Hal Haskins and Supe Lundsten, and guards Joey Hutton and Bob "Fish" Leiviska, were given as one of (if not THE) best college-level teams ever in the Upper Midwest couldn't be ignored. Plus, the vaunted Phillips 66ers seemed to want Vern desperately.

Finally, the Lakers showed a genuine interest in several ways, and the territorial draft would allow them to have first choice.

The new NBA itself provided an incentive that Vern found difficult to explain. "Somehow, even though the Lakers had had exceptional success, I felt as if I was getting in on the ground floor of something big."

The Rise of Professional Basketball

Fred ZOLLNER

At the time professional basketball was experiencing growing pains, yet its potential to challenge baseball and football in popularity was apparent to many enthusiasts from the first. The trick was how to publicize and organize this nascent giant.

The American Basketball League had been established in 1925, with franchises spreading out from Boston to New York to Chicago. The ABL was the first league to sign players to contracts of exclusivity, and it modified the rules to shift the game's emphasis away from strength toward finesse and speed.

In 1937 the ABL spawned the National Basketball League, which had nine teams, including two in Akron, Ohio (sponsored by Firestone and Goodyear). Players were given jobs with the sponsoring organizations and bonus money (like $5 or $10 a game) depending upon a team's success. The Oshkosh, Wisconsin, All Stars dominated the ABL from 1938 to 1942. The following three years the Fort Wayne Zollner Pistons were in the driver's seat. They played their games in armories, high school gymnasiums, dance halls, and even the back rooms of bars or beer joints. The team was owned by Fred Zollner, a Little Falls, Minnesota, native who had attended the University of Minnesota before starting a company that manufactured engine pistons. When Zollner moved the company from Duluth to Fort Wayne, Indiana, he started a basketball team in an effort to increase exposure for the firm.

Then, during the 1946-47 season, a player erupted upon the scene who would tear the league apart and raise its profile to the level of a marquee entertainment. That man was George Mikan. A one-time potential priest from Quigley Prep Seminary in Chicago, he became a basketball "giant" during his college years at DePaul. Mikan graduated in 1946, and the following autumn, as a 6-foot-10 rookie in the NBL, he carried his team, the Chicago American Gears, to the finals. Maurice White, the club's owner, considered his team to be so powerful, in fact, that he jerked it out of the NBL and boldly organized his own league of 24 teams for the 1947-48 season.

White's bid to rule the game of pro basketball failed miserably, however. It was called the National Professional Basketball League but it was underfunded from the start. The league only played eight games before it collapsed, and when it did, the Chicago American Gears folded with it. Mikan went into a pool of available players and was immediately picked by the Lakers.

Mikan's Laker Debut

During an interview in March 2005, Mikan recalled those two weeks of late November, 1947. "When I heard that the rights to me belonged to the Lakers, I think I actually shivered. I told my wife Pat—we had been married only a few months at the time—that when I thought of Minneapolis all that was on my mind was a New Year's Eve game I had played there with DePaul [December 31, 1945] against the University of Minnesota. We lost. But what I remembered

George Mikan

most vividly was how cold it was. In fact, I think I vowed never to return to that city if I could help it.

"Well, it turned out that I literally couldn't help it. The Lakers had rights to me and told me they would not give them up to anybody. Max Winter, Morris Chalfen, and Ben Berger were emphatic about that. They said they were sure we could come to a financial agreement that would satisfy me. A return to Minneapolis was inevitable. It was about six weeks earlier in the year than our frigid 1945 DePaul visit had been. I hoped for the best in terms of weather, as well as contract. My pal and attorney Stacey Osgood and I flew to Minneapolis on their tickets, proving how desperately they wanted me. Before we even started to talk to the Lakers, I had told Stacey what I was getting from the Chicago Gears [$12,000] before they cashed in their chips.

"In Winter's office in downtown Minneapolis the numbers were flying around, but not up where I thought they should be. I said I needed time to think. I knew they were hell bent to sign me. Heck, they needed me. Pollard was their biggest guy at 6-5. We concluded our conversation. We said we would go back to Chicago and think things over. Newspaperman Sid Hartman, who was helping them assemble a roster, was told to drive me to the airport. Well, Sidney took us on a wonderful tour of the lower half of the Twin Cities, showing us all the sights. It took long enough that we missed our flight, as Sid had planned. Turns out Winter had told him to do it. It was obvious they didn't want us to leave. Stacey and I had seen through the plan right away and got a great chuckle out of it. What it told us was they wanted us as badly as I had figured. And, really, we needed them, too. There was no second choice. The next morning, for $12,500, I signed. Joining Pollard, whom I had heard great things about, was a wonderful experience. We didn't jell immediately [the Lakers already had played four games, winning three and dropped four of five once Mikan arrived]. Once we did get it together, nobody could beat us."

The next year (1948-49) Mikan and Pollard won the NBL title with the Lakers, although the title has never been recognized by the NBA. The following year the NBL and the BAA merged to form the NBA, and because the rival BAA had teams in larger cities, under the direction of president Maurice Podoloff, it was considered the major partner, and its champion was granted the retroactive title.

Yet it was obvious to many observers that the on-court power of professional basketball was to be found not in the

BAA, but in three NBL teams—the Lakers, the Zollner Pistons, and the Rochester Royals. Podoloff also recognized that fact, which may explain why he worked so hard to entice all three of those teams into the newly formed NBA. Not only were they the best teams in the newly formed league, but in Mikan, Pollard, Bob Davies of the Royals, and John Pelkington of the Pistons, they had the star power that any new league needs to build a fan base.

Meanwhile, Maurice White's failed league, the NPBL, was reorganized under the same name in 1951. Schultz coached one of the teams, the St. Paul Lights, but they lasted only two months. Other members of the resurrected NPBL were Denver; Sheboygan, Wisconsin; and Waterloo, Iowa. Each had been part of a huge NBA along with the Lakers, but all three struggled financially.

When the NBA was a year old, in the summer of 1950, Sheboygan, Anderson, Denver, and Waterloo left to seek fortunes elsewhere. The St. Louis Bombers and Chicago Stags went broke. Shortly after the 1950-51 season began, the Washington Capitols franchise also closed its doors. That left ten teams in the NBA for its second season—the defending champion Lakers, Rochester, Fort Wayne, Syracuse, Boston, Baltimore, Philadelphia, New York, Indianapolis, and Milwaukee in addition to Minneapolis.

Mikkelsen Comes on Board

It was this conglomeration of new and old, prosperous and struggling, vibrant and resurrected teams, that formed the competitive milieu in the midst of which Mikkelsen began his professional career in the fall of 1949.

Mikan, Martin, Mikkelsen

Mikan remembered his introduction to the 20-year-old rookie, discounting their 1945 Christmas meeting in Chicago Stadium. "Mik and his minister father were brought down to the locker room after one of our first practices for the '49-50 season," recalled Mikan. "Owner Max Winter went wherever he wanted to, so he took them right into the doorway of the shower room to meet us.

"Well, the loud talk in the shower was rugged to say the least, profanity in abundance. I apologized for the cursing, feeling a bit embarrassed at the time. Reverend Mikkelsen put his hand on my shoulder and said, 'George, boys will be boys.' It relieved the tension. He was a great man," Mikan said.

"The same can be said for his son. In many ways he was like a younger brother to me. Right away I could see that Vern had a delightful sense of humor. Kind of sly. Many's the night that the two of us would go in one direction after a game or on an off day and the others would go in another.

I remember once in New York City we were walking fast on our way to a show. There were a couple of girls following us, moving as fast as they could with their high heels.

"Vern, trying to get rid of them, looked over his shoulder and asked, 'Are you girls out after hours?' They said, 'No, but we thought you might be out after *ours!*' Neither of us were the least bit interested."

When asked for an assessment of Vern's basketball contributions to the Lakers that first season, Mikan, three months prior to his death, said, "Well, first, he is one of my greatest friends. I would be hard pressed to think of anything negative. Second, Vern was simply ready, even eager, to be taught. He absorbed absolutely everything and had a desire to succeed that was apparent from the start. Kundla was trying a double-post offense after Vern arrived, with the two of us in the lane, high and low. After a short time, I said to Mik that there simply was not room for both of us down deep because with that narrow free-throw lane there just wasn't.

"John [Kundla] agreed and tried something which hadn't been done with a center before. He moved Mik out to Swede Carlson's right forward spot with Jim [Pollard] on the left. Mik was reluctant. Forward? He had always thought of himself as a center, that's all. In fact, Mik, I think, believed he was only around because Max had said I was to retire soon. Kundla and Ben Berger may also have hinted that to Vern. To get him to come with us, you know [rather than the Phillips 66ers]. I actually had no thoughts of retiring. Played five more years."

From the first Mikan could see the exceptional value of adding this kid of twenty from Hamline. "When Mik moved out to Swede's spot at right forward, it was a great adjustment for him. But what a front line it gave us with me between

Vern and Jim! As has been stated often, the term 'power forward' was born with Mik—a rebounder deluxe, a rugged
defender, and a strong team player," Mikan said.

Yes, just as Mikan revolutionized the position of a tall,
strong, hook-shooting center, and just as Pollard became a
small forward in a tradition later popularized by Michael
Jordan, most references to Mikkelsen are as the first of the
power-forward breed. Quite an accolade for a young man
who at twenty years of age was too young legally to sign his
first Laker contract. His father had to sign for him.

And what better credential for Mikkelsen than to have a
superstar like Mikan praise the newcomer's work ethic and
talent?

But what was Mik's attitude about playing alongside
Mikan? "There is no other way to say it than that I was in
awe of his every move. And why not? Here was a man named
the greatest player of the first half of the century, one who
rarely missed a game or a practice. [Mikan was unavailable
for only two games in his entire Laker career. In three playoff
games against Rochester in 1951, he played despite a pain-
ful, limiting, broken ankle.] It was because of Mikan that
they ruled out goal-tending during his days at DePaul; it was
because of him that they widened the free-throw lane from
six feet to 12 feet; it was because of Mikan that they came up
with the idea for a shot clock."

Mikan's impact on the development of Mikkelsen's game
was profound, but the role of Howie Schultz ought not to be
overlooked. First, he instilled in his Hamline protégé the will
to improve.

"Then there is the drill that Howie Schultz had me doing
endlessly when I got to Hamline," remembered Mikkelsen.

"It was named The Mikan Drill. It proved to be as valuable as it was boring and time consuming. Hook from the right side. Hook from the left side. Rebound your misses. Put them back up and in without lowering the basketball toward your body," Mikkelsen said. "George's coach at De Paul, Ray Meyer, made him do it over, and over, and over again. Howie did the same thing with me, until both my rebounding and shooting touch, especially with the hook, got pretty good. Many is the high school and college center who benefited by that drill." Among those who benefited, no doubt, is Kevin McHale, who played at Hibbing High School in northern Minnesota and went on to a stellar career at the University of Minnesota and with the Boston Celtics. (In 2003, McHale joined Lakers Mikan, Pollard, Slater Martin, Clyde Lovellette, Kundla, and Mikkelsen in the Basketball Hall of Fame in Springfield, Massachusetts.)

Mikan made such a profound impact on Mikkelsen's developing game during those years that it would be easy to underestimate the role played by the Lakers' coach, John Kundla. Yet Kundla's tireless emphasis on defense was the cornerstone upon which the team's unprecedented success was built.

"I had always insisted that defense wins championships," Kundla said. "And I saw immediately in Mik when he came with us that he took his defensive assignments very seriously. Give him someone to get after, and he did it with dedication some players lacked. I had coached McIntyre at Minnesota, and we beat DePaul, but I wondered if Jim would be tough enough for the rugged play in the NBA. I had heard how tough Mikkelsen was during his days at Hamline. Though I never saw him then, I found out in a hurry that it was true."

John Kundla

Kundla's is a story of Twin Cities basketball. He played as a kid in Northeast Minneapolis, in high school at Minneapolis Central, then at the University of Minnesota. After that he played independent ball at Shakopee. He coached De La Salle High School of Minneapolis to the state Catholic high school championship in 1944, beating St. Paul Cretin in the finals at Mankato. After two years in the Navy, where his basketball consisted of some ship-deck shooting at makeshift baskets, he spent a year at the University of Minnesota as an assistant to Dave Mac-

John Kundla

Millan (a situation later reversed with the Lakers). From his position as assistant with the Gophers, Kundla moved on to head coach at St. Thomas, where he posted an 11-11 record. The next year the Lakers beckoned.

Kundla at that time was thirty-one—extremely young to be thrust into such a high-visibility job. But he did things beyond anyone's expectations, eventually posting a 536-357 record including playoffs.

Mikkelsen admired him from the start. "He gave me a chance," he later said. The two became lifelong friends. Vern said, "John wanted what I was most able to give—rebounding, defense, setting picks, and making the correct pass inside. He asked me to play without fear of fouling, and I sure did that." Vern still holds the NBA record for

Mikkelsen called for a foul

fouling out of 127 games during his career (145 including playoffs). In ten regular seasons he picked up 2,812 fouls in all.

Kundla and Mikkelsen, who both declined to make the switch with the team to California in 1960 despite attractive offers to do so, were part of the double-post experiment along with Mikan. "George was right when he said it wasn't working," Kundla said. "It was too jammed up in there. When we moved Mik out to the forward spot Swede [Carlson] had played, he developed the overhead shot we asked him to, passed well to George inside and crashed the boards. Our rebounding made our fast break go, and we played some volleyball [with offensive rebounds] at the other end with Jim, Vern, and George."

In 1954 the Lakers beat the Knicks three straight in New York to secure a surprise championship. Counter-clockwise from front left: Max Winter, Dugie Martin, Ben Berger (owner), Vern Mikkelsen, John Kundla (coach), George Mikan, Clyde Lovellette, Jim Pollard, Jim Holstein.

Kundla identified the Lakers' NBA title in 1953-1954 over the Knicks and the one in 1950 over Syracuse as his two most satisfying championships. "The win over the Knicks because we split the first two at home, then went to New York for the next three. That arrangement had some of the Knicks claiming the series never would go back to Minneapolis, thinking they would win all three on their court. Well, we didn't go back to Minneapolis, but not because things went the way they had figured. We won all three in New York and held our victory celebration at the Copacabana." Whitey Skoog, who averaged just under four points a game during the regular season, came into his own in the Knicks series, causing New York coach Joe Lapchick to say, "We couldn't stop him."

"Against Syracuse in 1950," Kundla said, "they had earned home-court advantage with a better regular-season record.

We'd have to win at least once on their court and did so on Bobby Harrison's 40-footer as time ran out in the very first game. After that, we took all three at our place." ("Our place" actually was split with two at the St. Paul Auditorium and the sixth game, a fight- and foul-filled battle, at the Minneapolis Auditorium after the Sportsman's Show ended.)

The 1950 season concluded with Mikkelsen firmly entrenched in the monstrous front line, averaging 11½ points a game behind Mikan's 27 and Pollard's 15. Mikkelsen's rebounding totals were also right there with the other two, and the Lakers were roundly recognized as the best team ever in pro basketball.

What could happen next? Plotting in other camps had begun in earnest.

7

The Original Power Forward

B y the end of Vern Mikkelsen's second season with the Lakers, a new term had been added to the vocabulary of basketball: POWER FORWARD. But the development of this radical new offensive role was far from smooth.

The Lakers franchise has been a success on the court from the first, and Don "Swede" Carlson had been a part of it from the beginning. He was a starter in the very first game the Lakers played, on November 1, 1947, at Oshkosh, Wisconsin. On that occasion Jim Pollard led a Laker victory with 10 points, and Carlson secured it with a crucial field goal at the buzzer. Don Smith, a 6-2 ex-Gopher out of Minneapolis Roosevelt; Bob Gerber, at 6-5 (like Pollard), and Bill Durkee, a friend of Pollard's from Oakland, California, were the other starters.

Durkee was added to the team in rather casual fashion. "In August of 1947," he later recalled, "I was playing golf at Oakland's Tilden Park. At the 18th hole, I saw Jim Pollard waving at me to come over by the clubhouse. He was with an older man and told me that he had just signed to play with Minneapolis and wanted me to go with him. It was such an honor coming from Jim that I was proud to go. Jim was absolutely the finest basketball player in the world. No one had his combination of skill and grace."

When George Mikan joined the team later in the season the run toward true greatness began. The front line of Mikan, Carlson, and Pollard was soon joined by Jack Dwan out of Chicago Loyola and Herm Schaefer, who played collegiately at Indiana and as a professional at Fort Wayne and Indianapolis. With Jaros bringing instant offense off the bench, the victories began to pile up, and the team won its first championship. The next year the team won another title, this time in the BAA, after Arnie Ferrin from the University of Utah had been added to the mix.

"Swede" Carlson had begun his basketball career at Minneapolis Edison High and gone on to play for the Gophers at the University of Minnesota. After a stint of duty in World War II as a military pilot, he turned pro and became a star for the Chicago Stags of the BAA in 1946-47. His team lost to Philadelphia in the playoff finals that year, and during the off-season he was purchased (along with long-time pal Tony Jaros) by the fledgling Minneapolis Lakers franchise of the National Basketball League. They thus became the two charter members of the team that would later be widely referred to as professional basketball's "team of the decade."

The stage was set for Mikkelsen's professional debut as the season began in the fall of 1949. Yet it was far from clear at first how the athletic Dane would fit in with the already talented line-up.

From the time of Vern's first workout with the Lakers at the Minneapolis Athletic Club, he realized that subtle changes were taking place in a game he had known intimately for ten years through high school and college. Teams were drifting away from time-honored methods of defense. Through the 1940s, basketball was played with guards defensing forwards and forwards guarding guards. Yet the influx of taller players was gradually undermining that system and ineluctably replacing it with a system of matching up. Position names like left guard, right forward, and center began to give way to a number system ranging from a five man in the post through a four at the power forward, and on to a shooting forward, a shooting guard, and a point guard. The changes came slowly, but Mikkelsen found himself in the midst of them. Over the course of time, innocently, he was somewhat responsible for their success.

Faced with the challenge of utilizing two "big men" on the court simultaneously, Kundla at first attempted to develop a double pivot with Mikan and Mikkelsen. It soon became obvious that the experiment wasn't working. At that point Kundla made the radical decision to move Mikkelsen to the forward position. In an interview in October of 2004, Kundla said, "It was not easy to take Swede [Carlson] out of the line-up, him showing the fire in his belly and playing always with a business-like approach. But it seemed the realistic thing to do to put Mik in there alongside Pollard and Mikan."

"Realistic" and also extremely beneficial to the success of the Lakers. Carlson topped 6-foot-1 by just a fraction. Mikkelsen was 6-foot-7 and a robust 235 pounds. At that height, he was a half-foot taller than previous right forwards and much heavier. The unusual size and strength he brought to the position made itself felt every time he crashed the backboards in search of a rebound, executed a bruising defensive play, set a pick, or picked up a score after a teammate's miss. Carlson played the position as it had always been played, with solid defense and productive playmaking as the hallmarks. Mikkelsen changed all that.

Yes, a power forward. The word hadn't been coined yet, but that's what it was. And Mikkelsen fit the bill with both style and substance.

By the 1950-51 season, Bob Harrison and Slater ("Dugie") Martin had also moved into starting roles. They had been drafted in 1949 with Mikkelsen but usually came off the bench to spell team captain Schaefer and Ferrin, who was to leave the pro game after only three seasons. Schaefer and Carlson also soon retired, the latter becoming a basketball coach and later the athletic director at Columbia Heights, Minnesota, High School.

Stall Tactics

With Harrison and Martin as starters, the 1950-1951 season was developing smoothly for the Lakers. In fact, for the previous eleven and a half months the team had racked up twenty-nine straight victories at home. Their opponent for

Carl Bennett

the Thanksgiving Eve game, Fort Wayne, had lost its previous seven games in Minneapolis. A crowd of more than seven thousand filled the seats at the Minneapolis Auditorium, looking forward to yet another comfortable victory.

Carl Bennett and the Pistons had a different idea in mind.

Bennett had long been an astute observer of how professional basketball was developing. In fact, his experience in the world of sport was impressive by any measure. Early in his career he had been a crack first-baseman for the Fort

Wayne Zollner Pistons' nationally famous fast-pitch soft-ball team, and he later became a recruiter for Zollner's pro basketball team. Among the many stars he recruited during that spell were Carlisle ("Blackie") Towery out of Western Kentucky, George Yardley out of Stanford (who signed for $9,500), and Bobby McDermott of the New York Traveling Celtics. (Like many players in the NBA's more-recent years, McDermott turned pro right out of Flushing, New York, High School.)

Bennett later coached the Pistons, served as general manager, and then took a position on the board of governors of the National Basketball Association. He even served for a time as president of the league.

It was while he was coaching during the 1946-47 season that Bennett got his first look at 6-foot-10 George Mikan. A year later, when Minneapolis got its franchise, Mikan began to work with the multi-talented Pollard on both ends of the court, and the duo was almost too much. "They were enough to make you lay awake at night wondering how to combat them," Bennett said in a 2004 interview.

Bennett made his first efforts to do something dramatic about the dominance of the Laker team in 1950, when he was serving on the NBA's Executive Council. Along with fellow council member Ned Irish of New York, he strongly advocated widening the free-throw lane from six to twelve feet.

This change was not instituted until two years later, and meanwhile, Bennett's Pistons still had to face Mikan, Pollard, and Mikkelsen on the court. Bennett was well aware that it was not only Mikan's dominance in the paint that was giving the Lakers such an edge over opposing teams. No,

Mikkelsen at work against the Knicks' Vince Boryla and
Connie Simmons, ca 1958

the Lakers had made a dramatic change in the very way the
game was played by moving Mikkelsen out to right forward.
"There, Mikkelsen did things never before seen at that position on a court, at least not to the extent Vern did them: setting powerful picks, crashing both backboards for rebounds,
and playing tough defense from opening tip to final buzzer.
He did some fouling, and fouling out, but that was nothing
compared to the way he influenced, in a demoralizing way,
another team's offense. He was a perfect fit for the job John

wanted done. He became a prototype for what has become a power forward standard in the basketball business."

But Bennett was not one to give up a fight easily. And when Pistons' coach Murray Mendenhall made a passionate plea for a strategy other than the team's usual run-and-shoot style to take the Lakers by surprise on that Thanksgiving Eve of 1950, general manager Bennett agreed to give it a shot.

A blow-by-blow account of this famous non-fight on the court can begin with the opening trip down the court by the Pistons. The Lakers assumed their normal defensive positions, Pollard, Mikan, and Mikkelsen under the basket awaiting enemy thrusts and Slater Martin and Harrison out near the free-throw circle ready to disrupt Piston offensive plans. But a strange thing occurred. Fort Wayne center Larry Foust stood out near the center line with the ball under one arm. He remained there as the spectators began to fume. Afterward, Fred Schaus, a Fort Wayne forward, said, "They didn't come out, so we didn't go in." Even when the Pistons fell behind 13-11 at the half and by similarly slight margins until the final minute, they stayed outside with the ball whenever they had it and were able to do so. Kundla criticized the Piston plan, saying, "If that is basketball, I don't want any part of it."

With just under ten seconds remaining, and trailing 18-17, Fort Wayne had exactly what it had gone into the game looking for—a chance to win. Foust took a pass some twelve feet from the basket with five seconds left and threw up a last-gasp field-goal try. "I think George even got a piece of it," Mikkelsen later recalled. In any case, it went in. It was only the eighth field goal of the game, but it won the game for the Zollner Pistons. Mikan finished with fifteen of the eighteen Laker points in the setback, with Bobby Harrison adding two free throws and Pollard one.

At the time, this game was viewed in many quarters as simply frightful. Yet it also made it crystal clear that significant changes would be required to maintain the viability of basketball as a spectator sport. This dreadful exercise in "winning ugly" would eventually lead to the formation of new rules that would benefit the game immensely.

The stall tactics of Fort Wayne that day resulted in the lowest scoring game in NBA history. Strange as it may seem, a few years later, on March 19, 1956, the Lakers defeated St. Louis 133-75—the largest margin of victory in NBA playoff history, thus placing themselves at both ends of the NBA point parade.

Among basketball executives the Piston plan of November 22, 1950, immediately came under close scrutiny. NBA president Maurice Podoloff said, "I don't want anything like that to ever happen again." Four years later, the league was to make a decision that would ensure that it would not be repeated.

"For more than two years," Mikkelsen said, "I would have conversations with Eddie Gottlieb [owner of the Philadelphia Warriors] and Danny Biasone [the Syracuse owner]. Each kept insisting that there should be a time limit put on teams to put up a shot while on offense. I would see each of them at games, sitting in the stands with stopwatches, timing each offensive advance down-court.

"Amazingly, each came up with the same answer: twenty-four seconds is what should be allowed for a team to hold the ball from start to finish [a shot at the basket] in each possession." A clock was to prevent teams from holding the basketball for long periods when facing a superior opponent, especially the powerful Lakers.

Another strategy used by Warrior coach Gottlieb at the time against the Laker powerhouse was to foul Mikan each time the team came down court. "One shot [free throw] instead of two points," he said. At the time, a non-shooting foul always resulted in just one free throw. However, Mikan's eighty percent success from the free-throw line wrecked that strategy.

Teams also began to search for tall forward-type players "like Bob Pettit, Arnie Johnson, and Harry Gallatin," said Mikkelsen. "It became big guy against big guy at my position. No more advantages for me of four or five inches over my opponent."

All in all, the changes that were made to the game to maintain competitiveness during the years of Laker dominance were considerable. Goal-tending was gone; so, too, the narrow free-throw lane and the opportunity to stall minutes off the clock without a shot being taken. Foul disqualifications came at six rather than five, keeping stars in the game longer. Zone defenses were outlawed.

Bennett led the cheers when his boss introduced a new mode of team transportation. Zollner bought a Douglas DC-3 in 1952 to move his Pistons from game to game—a first in sports history.

Also under Bennett, Fort Wayne, in 1953, was the first to make a multi-faceted spectacle of hosting the All-Star Game. Governor George Craig proclaimed it Indiana Basketball Week. Sportscasters and writers were flown in from the East to broaden publicity outlets. All in all, seventy-five members of the media showed up, including fourteen radio stations, which was completely unprecedented for such an event. Moreover, the inclusion around the court of some half-dozen cameras for television and newsreels, prompted the NBA to sign its first television contract (with Dumont) a year later. Developments were flooding into the pro game. America was paying more attention week by week.

Yet the hoopla surrounding the Fort Wayne All-Star game would soon be a distant memory. A rush of the league into larger cities struck a death knell for the Piston franchise in Fort Wayne. Only 2,200 spectators watched a home game against the Lakers on March 19, 1957. Mikkelsen said, "As wildly successful and entertaining as the 1953 All-Star Game was both for us participants and those watching, it was equally disappointing to see the small crowd four years later."

Bennett said, "Fred claimed that he simply had to move to the market, and that turned out to be Detroit. Even with a $2.50 top ticket, we could not continue to attract customers at Fort Wayne. Fred considered Louisville, but wound up selecting Detroit despite its poor record of support for the sport."

An era had ended that, as Bennett insisted, saw more alterations in the game of basketball than any other time period. During that same period the league had fluctuated from a high of seventeen to a low of eight franchises.

Jim Pollard and the Slam Dunk

No discussion of the changes that came about between 1945 and 1955 would be complete without mention of the rise, fall, and resurrection of the slam dunk.

Jim Pollard, Mikkelsen's teammate and singing partner, was the epitome of the gravity-defying basketball standout who had the ability to dunk. To understand what has been the significance of the signature "shot" of basketball, one must first learn about Pollard.

Pollard grew up in Oakland, California, and was a high school star at Tech High in 1939 and 1940. In 1941 he was a

member of Stanford's freshman team, ineligible then for varsity competition by NCAA regulations (later he said that he felt that he "missed a whole year"). As a sophomore in 1942, he helped Stanford to the NCAA title.

He served, and played, in the Coast Guard before joining the Oakland Bittners, one of America's top semi-pro teams. (These teams played in the Amateur Athletic Union, but the players were given "jobs" by the organizations they played for.) He also wore the uniform of the San Diego Dons, a similar club, while "waiting for a chance to represent his country in the 1948 Olympics," as his widow Arilee was to say later.

Once the Lakers had acquired Kundla as coach in 1947— he doubted whether the game could be successful in Minneapolis and turned down the job three times before accepting—the organization turned its attention to signing Pollard. Once they'd achieved that second objective, the success of the franchise was assured. Pollard was the team's tallest player at 6-5 (a situation soon to change with the addition of Mikan) and he immediately earned the respect of both teammates and foes with his all-round talent.

The dunk had been a highlight-reel accompaniment to the game of basketball and nothing more than that for years. It was done in pre-game drills by the Lakers and others but not in games. The barnstorming New York Rens of the early 1930s were said to have plenty of players who could jump high enough to send a ball on a downward trip through the net, but they did not do so with the gusto to be seen later.

Arthur Daley of the *New York Times* coined the term "dunk" after watching an itinerant company team from Kansas called the McPherson Oilers in 1936. The McPherson version of a layup in warming up for a game consisted of 6-9 Willard Schmidt and 6-8 Joe Fortenberry slamming a ball down into the hoop—"like the dunking of a doughnut" as Daley put it. The dunk had been named.

Ten years later, word drifted east out of Los Angeles, and Pollard heard it, about Jackie Robinson's aerial displays around the hoop. As everyone knows, Robinson later became the first African-American to play major-league baseball (pushing Howie Schultz off first base at Dodger Stadium), but at that time he was flying high in basketball for the professional Los Angeles Red Devils. At UCLA his jumping ability also propelled him to a collegiate record in the long-jump, and on the court the barely 6-foot Robinson was one of the first basketball players famous for his ability to dunk.

Pollard brought a similar gift to the NBA but was loathe to use it in a game, believing it to be demeaning to a defender.

In practice, however, he wowed his Laker teammates by taking off from about the free-throw line and sailing to the hoop to slam down the ball. "But in 10 years of professional ball," said widow Arilee, "I can't remember him embarrassing an opponent that way."

The dunk was illegal in college basketball in the decade between 1967 and 1977, at least partially because of Kareem Abdul-Jabbar's slamming at UCLA. Many of the best players seemed to shun the maneuver. Elgin Baylor, Oscar Robertson, Mikan, Pollard and Jerry West (to name a few) preferred to go high and then "finger roll" the ball into the net.

Wilt Chamberlain popularized the dunk in professional ball, using it as many as two dozen times in a game. With the Philadelphia 76ers during the late 1960s, Chamberlain teamed with Chet Walker and Lucious Jackson to form an impressive front line—the first to be spoken of in the same breath as the Mikan-Pollard-Mikkelsen trio of the Lakers.

Pollard retired in 1955, and in the 1956 playoffs, Mikkelsen remembers, the Lakers did something "that blew my mind. We were playing the [St. Louis] Hawks in the playoffs and wasted a 19-point lead in losing the first game. Then we beat them 133-75 in the second game, biggest spread I'm told in playoff history as all ten of us were in double figures. Winning by 58 points, we all thought, I guess, that we were invincible once again. Turned out that wasn't so. The Hawks won the deciding third game by one point on two late free-throws. George played well, averaging in double figures I'm sure [actually 10.5] but we weren't the same without Jim." The Big Three had been 1-2-3 in points and rebounds for the Lakers for an unprecedented five straight years.

Original Laker Pollard retired with 6,522 points in a professional career that stretched through 497 games. He was blessed by his peers often with the accolade of "best all-round player"—a tribute awarded in 1950 through a vote of the NBA's top players. He later coached at LaSalle College and in the pros.

Pollard was known to many of his fans as the Kangaroo Kid, but he is perhaps best known among basketball insiders as The Man Who Wouldn't Dunk.

8

Lute Olson Is Watching

Vern Mikkelsen's rise from country-boy unknown to professional standout offers intriguing parallels to other professional sporting careers.

Phil Jackson is a prime example. A preacher's kid like Mikkelsen, he was raised in Williston, North Dakota, the son of two Pentecostal ministers, Charles and Elizabeth Jackson. Being a preacher's kid, everything "good" was expected of him, and as a result, he occasionally became a rebel of sorts. Had he sought one, Jackson would have found a role model in Mikkelsen, a minister's son who rode basketball out of small-town America into the big leagues. Jackson played basketball and also pitched for the baseball team at the University of North Dakota. His college coach, Bill Fitch, suggested he might like AAU ball, but Jackson, like Mikkelsen, elected to try the NBA instead. He played thirteen seasons, became the league's winningest coach (in victory percentage), and even campaigned for a rule eliminating fouling out. That is something Mikkelsen would have liked—he fouled out of more pro games than any other player in history.

Lute Olson may be taken as another case in point. The winningest basketball coach in Pac-Ten history at the

Phil Jackson on the mound for the
University of North Dakota

University of Arizona, Olson is among countless men and women who grew up in the Midwest knowing about, and being inspired by, what the kid from the rutabaga fields of Askov did in professional sports. When Lute was four, his father, Albert, died of a stroke. He was forty-seven. Lute's mother, Alinda, was forced to sell the farm, and Lute, a third-generation immigrant Norwegian, moved with her to Mayville, North Dakota, where he excelled in all sports as a youngster, particularly in basketball. The Mayville High coach, Ole Odney, was Olson's first basketball hero. Unfortunately, by the time Lute entered high school, Odney had moved on to college coaching at Augustana in Sioux Falls, South Dakota, and Harold Poier became Lute's coach. Olson played each sport in season at Mayville, starting with his freshman year—football, baseball, basketball, and track, where he threw the shot and discus.

After his junior year, a traumatic event altered Olson's life. An older sister, Kathleen, had been studying in Minneapolis to become a nurse. When Kathleen landed a job as a nurse in Grand Forks, Lute's mother insisted that the senior-to-be accompany her to Grand Forks so they could all "become a family again." Lute recoiled at the idea of leaving friends and teammates. But he went.

Lute had watched an older brother, Marvin, play out his career as a prep for Odney at Mayville, and he had anticipated doing the same himself. It didn't work out that

Lute Olson

way. "My senior year at Grand Forks [1952] was more than I could have imagined," he said. During his senior year Olson helped Grand Forks under Fritz Engel win a state championship in basketball. Then he weighed his options much as Mikkelsen had done seven years earlier. "I considered the University of North Dakota right there in Grand Forks," Olson said. "But being a small-town kid, I thought I would be better off in a little smaller school, so I picked Augsburg." There he played four years of football and basketball and was on the baseball team as a senior.

"I knew a little bit about Mikkelsen's success at Hamline. When I got to Augsburg I could watch his emergence as the very first power forward with the Lakers. He concentrated on defense and rebounding, something I have urged my players to do through my years of coaching," Olson said.

"In following Vern's career, I noted similarities to my own. He was from a little town and so was I. He was in band and chorus in high school in addition to athletics, and so was I. We both picked small colleges to continue our education. The church was a big part of his life and it was in mine, too. He was big and strong and I—well, we weren't *exactly* alike, you know," he said with a grin.

Olson has sailed in some high-test waters since serving five years as the high school basketball coach at Two Harbors, Minnesota (1956-61). He began his remarkable college coaching run at the University of Arizona in 1983, when he was 48, and eventually surpassed even UCLA's legendary John Wooden in career victories.

In 2006, Olson's Wildcats, during their seemingly inevitable annual trip to the NCAA tournament, boosted his career victory total to 761, putting him behind only one active coach—Bob Knight. During that time Olson has had great success in grooming college athletes for the rigors of the NBA. Sean Elliott and Steve Kerr head a parade of former U of A players that made it into the pros. In 2006 there were, among others, Mike Bibby of Sacramento, Jason Terry of Dallas, Gilbert Arenas of Washington, Luke Walton of the Lakers, Channing Frye of New York, Damon Stoudamire of Memphis, and Richard Jefferson of New Jersey. Each insists that while in school at Arizona, they were inspired by Olson to be professional in all walks of life, not only in their approach to basketball. Luke Walton's father, Bill, who was an NBA superstar with the Portland Trailblazers and more recently a self-appointed spokesman for the game of basketball, offers Olson high praise by likening him to Walton's own college coach—John Wooden.

Olson is the only native North Dakotan in the Basketball Hall of Fame in Springfield. In his 2002 acceptance speech, he told of two tragedies in his early life that transformed his future. The first was the death of his father. The second was when his brother Amos, who had returned home from college to run the farm, was killed in a tractor accident. Had that not happened, he said, "I would probably still be on that farm. The work ethic of my mother and my father was ingrained in my sister, my brothers, and me at an early age. I never considered any other occupation. Coaching has never been a job to me—it has been a labor of love." So, as was the case with Mikkelsen, an accidental high school occurrence shaped Olson's life.

When Olson lost his wife, Bobbi, to cancer, he donated $1 million in her name to the Arizona Cancer Center at the University of Arizona.

Lute's fame has led to an odd musical development. The Augsburg Centennial Singers, a group of largely retired Twin Citians (most of whom attended Augsburg), travel far and wide to spread the good news of the Bible in song and extol the merits of the college as well. Olson is cited generously as a former Augsburg athlete who while in school sang with a group called the Augsburg Quartet. Its alumni include some present-day Centennial Singers.

Air Travel Changes the Game

During his years with the Lakers, Mikkelsen saw the many changes in the game described in earlier chapters. But perhaps no development in the sport was more revolutionary than the one that took place well above the ground.

Fred Zollner of the Pistons actually started the trend of flying to and from games. The Lakers and others remained earth-bound for several more years. "In my first five years in the league," Mik said, "we traveled darn-near exclusively by train. In a few emergencies we flew Braniff, with pilots such as Maurice Taylor."

"As a joke," Mikkelsen said, "we used to call our many Laker trips 'flying by train.' I guess because we slept away as many of the hours as we could despite the cramped quarters. As mostly big guys, the sleepers weren't much good to us. George especially had trouble, being the biggest of us all. I remember one trip in particular, riding a train from Minneapolis to Chicago and then changing to another train and on to New York. We had hurried from a game at the Minneapolis Auditorium to get to the train station to catch the overnight to Chicago. George always got the biggest sleeper because of his longer legs, but this particular night his bed had not been properly made up. He told the porter to re-do his bed while we went to the dining car for an hour or so. When we got back to our sleeping quarters, there was the porter waiting for George with his hand stretched out in front of him. He wanted a tip. George looked at him and said, with fun-loving sarcasm, 'I'll give you a tip: Get out of this racket.' Such travel made us all a little irritable. Because that just wasn't like George. He did it to make us laugh, which he often did. I'm sure he tipped the fellow out of our sight.

"Another time there was an overtime game in Rochester. We learned that our train was late in arriving. We could still catch it if we hurried. We left the locker room without showering or changing clothes. We got to the station just in time to catch our train to head out. Through some mix-up in tickets, we all had to sleep in upper bunks in a very old car. We hung our uniforms over the rods in the upper level to dry out. When we got out of our berths in the morning, we were pretty smelly and not very popular with other passengers," he said.

"It reminded me of a time in college when we had played in an invitational in Los Angeles on New Year's Eve. We watched the Rose Bowl Parade and game and left for St. Paul that night. We got snowbound in Green River, Wyoming, for four days. In the pros, with games scheduled, we just couldn't do that.

"Another night, when I was with the Lakers, we could get only as far as Milwaukee from Minneapolis by train on our way to a game in Fort Wayne. Snow was piled up extremely high. So Fred Zollner was going to send his plane to Milwaukee to take us to Fort Wayne. John [Kundla] had been suffering from a bad stomach and he had gone to the dining car to drink some milk. He wasn't with the rest of us in our car when the Piston guy came in to round us up to take us to the airport. When we got off the train it was finally able to move, and we saw John through the dining-car window drinking his milk. He didn't know we had all left the train.

"We got to Fort Wayne in Zollner's plane in time for the game. John, on the train, did not get there by the time the game started. So Jim Pollard took over as acting coach. At halftime we were ahead. When the second half started, we heard the fans giving a large cheer. Kundla had arrived! He had a big overcoat on and was walking toward the bench carrying his suitcase. As luck would have it, he took over the coaching of the team, and we proceeded to lose the game. The fans were delighted. In the locker room we

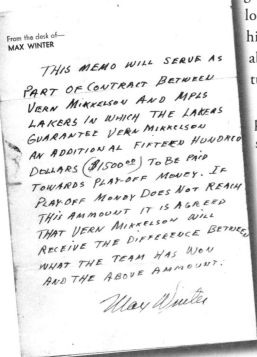

From the desk of—
MAX WINTER

THIS MEMO WILL SERVE AS PART OF CONTRACT BETWEEN VERN MIKKELSON AND MPLS LAKERS IN WHICH THE LAKERS GUARANTEE VERN MIKKELSON AN ADDITIONAL FIFTEEN HUNDRED DOLLARS ($1500.00) TO BE PAID TOWARDS PLAY-OFF MONEY. IF PLAY-OFF MONEY DOES NOT REACH THIS AMMOUNT IT IS AGREED THAT VERN MIKKELSON WILL RECEIVE THE DIFFERENCE BETWEEN WHAT THE TEAM HAS WON AND THE ABOVE AMMOUNT.

Max Winter

A playoff bonus

gave John a bad time for losing Jim's lead. Much to his distress, John heard about that bit of misfortune for a long time."

Traveling by train was particularly disturbing for some of the taller players. "For guys 6-5 like Pollard, up to George's 6-10, the sleepettes, as I think they were called, were like spending the nights in coffins," Vern said.

Coach Kundla wearied of the game-after-game necessity of train travel. "Taking me away from my family too much," he said. Air travel was rapidly becoming a vital necessity.

Once air travel had become safe and affordable, it radically expanded the competitive possibilities for western cities, thrusting them more squarely within the pro sports spectrum. Previously, everything that happened in sports did so east of a line running from Chicago to St. Louis. "Go west, young athlete" had meant all the way to Green Bay, Wisconsin. As the Lakers were pushing their way into the basketball picture, Cleveland took the National Football League to Los Angeles. A decade later, the Giants and Dodgers transplanted baseball from the East to the West Coast. In order to ford the Mississippi River, professional sports had to climb above the clouds.

Those who had originally wanted to establish the Lakers franchise from 1940 to 1945 had been advised repeatedly by eastern interests that even Minneapolis was too far west, and that the winter weather there was too cold for the city to join the league. But bold adventurers Max Winter and Ben Berger would not be denied. They secured the collapsing Detroit franchise for $15,000 to solidify entry into the picture. The Lakers roared to immediate prominence, winning six championships in their first seven seasons.

Unfortunately, during those early years only those fans who actually attended the games got the opportunity to see this powerful new entertainment package. Little by little television secured a place in the living rooms of sports-minded Americans, and by 1955, Sunday afternoon Laker telecasts were being carried in Minneapolis, Duluth, Austin, and Rochester in Minnesota, and also to Eau Claire, Wisconsin, and Fargo, North Dakota. Such an effort was considered the best in the NBA. But by the time television really took hold, the Lakers were moving to Los Angeles.

But whether live or merely televised, the success of the NBA during the 1950s made it clear that there was a new "huge athlete" on the scene, bigger than Babe Ruth in girth and height and as powerfully built as Minnesota's football colossus Bronko Nagurski. The Mikan-Mikkelsen type basketball player had come into fashion.

To wit, an anonymous poem was written after a Minneapolis-locale interview was held with Mikkelsen:

A BIG MAN

A big man doesn't have to be a giant as to size,
A truly big man must know when to talk or turn his eyes,
A great man isn't one who fights when someone drops a hat,
A truly good man must at times give in to this and that,
A big man must know how to lose when lesser humans win,
He must be gay in spite of woe, to show he's genuine,
He must be kind and tolerant and honest all the way,
And face the world with faith in God, to help him every day,
He must have love within his heart,
Not hate or jealousy,
And though his size may be minute,
        A real big man is he.

9

Danish Pastry, and a Wedding

Calling Verner Mikkelsen "The Great Dane" may be a bit presumptuous.

Plus, he doesn't like it.

The term has been used before. Quite often. Lauritz Melchior earned that kind of respect with his gallant Metropolitan Opera tenor voice. Bert Thorvaldsen in the early nineteenth century sculpted an unforgettable statue of Jesus Christ. Tycho Brahe founded modern astronomy way back to the sixteenth century. Karen Blixen, a baroness, writing under the pseudonym Isak Dinesen, was famous for *Out of Africa* and *Seven Gothic Tales*. Niels Bohr was a pioneer in atomic physics. Well, you get the idea. Vern, in his own modest way, suggested he might be called "The Fairly Great Dane"!

Vern watched a 1952 Copenhagen performance of Carl Brisson, celebrated singing star of stage, screen and radio, who was knighted by the kings of both Denmark and Sweden. And, in February of 1954, on a Laker trip to New York City, he saw Copenhagen's own Victor Borge in *A Comedy in Music* at the John Golden Theatre.

Also, from Vern's standpoint, there are two names not nearly as well known as some others, names which made his excitement level rise. Niels-Henning Oersted Pedersen—who died in 2005 in Denmark—was an institution to those who closely followed jazz. Mikkelsen, whose love of music paralleled his love of basketball, followed Oersted's career from the beginning, when he rocketed to fame in 1962 as a bass player with Copenhagen's well-known Montmartre jazz group, playing in a club of the same name. Later he played with Miles Davis, Oscar Peterson, Chet Baker, Dizzy Gillespie, and others of that ilk. Danish Radio's Big Band was an integral part of Oersted's life for almost twenty years. And there was Ralph Andrist, a Dane whose mother preached to him that farming was the only productive work for a man (much as Vern's parents had indicated, almost silently, that he could be a good preacher some day). Andrist became renowned for his book *The Long Death: The Last Days of the Plains Indians*.

Did being Danish make Vern reluctant to get married, give up his independence? Did he see it as relinquishing his freedom? From the day he joined the Lakers in 1949 until June 18, 1955, Mik was the lone single Laker, a situation that the wives of some other Lakers seemed dedicated to alter—for the better, they all thought. Yes, it was the other "altar" they had in mind for our Vern. "I took it as quite a compliment," Mikkelsen said, "and I did meet a lot of nice girls because of it. I just wasn't in any hurry."

Arilee Pollard, widow of Jim, remembers those times: "He was such a nice young man, a perfect gentleman, and quite good looking. So, yes, we did have in mind the improving of his life through marriage. Some of us looked at it as an obligation even."

Vern said, "God has smiled down upon me many, many times in my life, but never so graciously as one day in the fall of 1954. Joe and Shirley Hutton [Vern always used Joe to mean Joe Jr. and "Coach" to mean Joe Sr.] introduced me to Jean. She was a buyer for The Bridal Shop. We hit it off immediately. I learned something new from her every day."

In the spring of 1954, Mikkelsen had spent a week with his parents in Rosenberg, Nebraska, "where my dad was serving a church. He helped me finish my master's work so I could get my degree in psychology in the winter of 1954-55. Jean was there when I was presented my degree at the University of Minnesota. It was about then that we decided to get married the following June.

Finally, in mid-June of 1955, after Vern's sixth season as a Laker, the long-awaited wedding ceremony took place, at Green Lake Lutheran Camp Chapel near Spicer, Minnesota. Mik and Jean walked down the aisle, and Vern's father officiated, along with Reverend Alvin Nygaard. "We had a big turnout at the ceremony." Mikkelsen. said. "Coach Hutton was there along with many of my Hamline classmates and teammates and of course Laker friends, too. It was a perfect wedding, well worth the wait."

Reverend Nygaard was pastor of the First Methodist Church in Willmar, which was Jean's home church. Vern's attendants were his brother-in-law Joe Jackson (Hertha's husband) as best man and Jim Pollard as groomsman. Ushers were fellow-Lakers Dick Schnittker and Joe Hutton, Jr. The afternoon ceremony saw the chapel decorated with garlands of huckleberry interspersed with large daisies, compliments of Irv Hanson, Vern's new father-in-law, who owned a nursery in Willmar. (Earlier he had taught school.)

Vern and Jean on their wedding day

The organist was A. M. Wisness, superintendent of schools at Willmar. Grayson Osteraas sang "A Wedding Prayer." The music, naturally, was of particular importance to Mik. Anne Hanson, Jean's sister, was maid of honor and Patricia Price was the bridesmaid. After a bridal dinner at Hultgren's Lodge near Green Lake, the newlyweds left for a wedding trip to—where else?—Otis Lodge of Grand

Rapids, where Vern had worked summers during his youth. He said, "We knew we would have a more elaborate honeymoon later."

The last line of the wedding report in the Willmar newspaper read, "Mr. Mikkelsen is captain of the Minneapolis Laker basketball team."

Vern, Jean, and son Tom

To Jean and Vern, son Tom was born June 18, 1958, and son John in August of 1963. To son Tom and his wife Jennifer, Vern's grandsons Kyler and Caden were born February 3, 2001, and February 20, 2003, respectively. Each development strengthened Vern's sense of family unity, "all joined together with and under God," he said. Still, all his life there was an adventurous side to be satisfied.

He said, "I have been fortunate to do many interesting things in my life, travel considerably, study and observe tons of fascinating people. Victor Borge, as you might guess because of the Danish connection, was a personal favorite entertainer of mine."

On Mik's extended odyssey, there were other brushes, too, with famous people. He was on the set, along with other basketball friends, to watch Marilyn Maxwell and Kirk Douglas star in the making of the movie *Champion*. When he spent a college-graduate week at the Lexington Hotel in New York as the West All-Stars prepared to meet the East in the spring of 1949, after his final season at Hamline, he spent considerable time in the Lexington people-watching and reading. "I sat in the lobby every day near Arthur

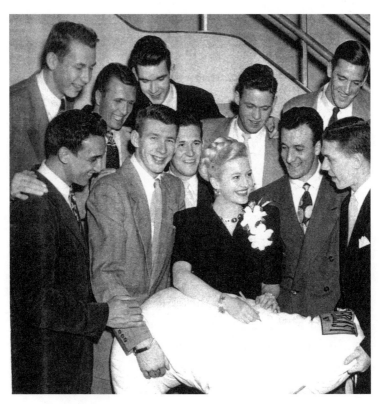

Vern in New York (upper left) among fans of Marilyn Maxwell

Godfrey, who seemed to be content just to do what I was doing.

"When we were in New York once to play the Knicks, I ran into and talked to Perry Como, who said he had seen me play a lot. He was a strong basketball follower. I was surprised that he recognized me and opened a conversation. It was apparent he was quite a fan of the Celtics! He lived in Boston."

Mikkelsen concedes that not all of his travel experiences went famously. "I remember one time in New York City," he said. "For years I had always tuned in my radio on New Year's Eve and listened to the Times Square report of the arrival of the New Year at midnight. I always wanted to be there for the big event. And so it happened that on December 31, 1951, we played a game at Madison Square Garden. I decided I had enough time to get over to Times Square for the big event. It was about 11:30 when the game ended, but I hurriedly got dressed and ran the four blocks to Times Square. A huge number of revelers had gathered to wait for the countdown. I turned the corner from Sixth Avenue and began working my way through the mob of people. Wouldn't you know, a drunk picked that exact moment to throw up on my left shoe. I didn't have time to even holler at him as I turned to watch the 10-9-8-7-6-5-4-3-2-ONE. When I looked for the guy who threw up on my shoe, I couldn't find him. So I took off the shoe and carried it back to the hotel. The doorman, thinking I was a bit inebriated, I suppose, made a smart remark about my shoe. But I ran up to my room, into the bathroom, and scrubbed off my shoe the best I could. Some people think that is my best Laker story. I'll admit I think about it every New Year's Eve."

Along with Mikkelsen's chance meetings with Perry Como, a bunch of the Lakers appeared on the *Steve Allen Show*—the one that preceded Johnny Carson's run. "Steve pretended he was playing basketball against us, using a stepladder, which was positioned so that the audience couldn't see it. I was told that people in their living rooms at home thought it was hilarious. After the show I got to spend considerable time with his two new singers, Eydie Gorme and Steve Lawrence. They got married a year or two later and I saw them many times on TV."

The Lakers went back to Minneapolis and Vern scarcely had time "to charge the batteries before Paul Jorgensen and I loaded up some clean clothes and left for New York. In no time I was on a ship called the *Stavengsfjord* headed for Norway. Paul, who like me had a Danish minister father, talked me into it. I had told Paul I was staying at the University of Minnesota to finish work on my master's. He thought it would be a good idea for me to attend the University of Oslo instead, as all of my credits would be transferable. So I bought into it.

"Paul and I left New York on June 1, 1952, and spent ten wonderful days on board ship with about 250 other interesting students from all over. We spent six weeks at the University of Oslo, and thrown into the mix were some great side-trips around Norway. A highlight was the Fourth of July celebration, which surprised me, in Oslo."

Mikkelsen also did a favor for Max Winter in addition to his studying. "Max wanted to know if there were any potential NBA players from other countries participating in the Summer Olympics at Helsinki. So I flew down. The trip to Helsinki was great, but too short. Not surprisingly, I saw no NBA super prospects. I hurried back to Oslo. When my classes were finished there, Paul and I bought motorcycles and proceeded to tour Europe, another month of fabulous sights and sounds. We ended our trip in London. I had to get back to the Laker workouts. In Helsinki I had toured night clubs with a native Finn, Sulu Herala, who knew his way around the most interesting places. Later, he was with me to see a show by singer Carl Brisson in Copenhagen.

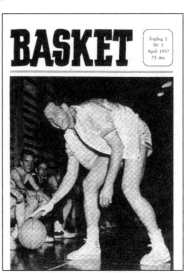

Vern on the cover of a Swedish basketball magazine, 1957

"In Denmark, I was able to do some research on my family history. Both Paul and I spoke Danish before learning English, so we got along well. On the trip home I had lots to reminisce about concerning Germany, Austria, Italy, Switzerland, France, and Czechoslovakia. Not too long after, I was in Paul's wedding in Blue Earth, Minnesota."

After Vern and Jean were married, along came another opportunity to explore the world in an unusual way. "It was after the 1957 season had ended. Jean and I were still without children. We were pretty much footloose and able to do what we wanted. One morning the phone rang. It was the U.S. State Department asking if I could go to Sweden for three months to coach the Swedish Olympic basketball team. It didn't sound as if the invitation included Jean, so I politely told them, 'No thank you.' Ten minutes later, Jean asked who had called and I told her. She said it sounded like something she would love to do, so she called the State Department people back. She was told that something might be worked out for both of us to go. Later that day we were called to say it was OK if Jean went, too.

"We were very excited. But we had to leave in just two days for Washington, D.C. and a briefing." By April, the two of them were in Stockholm, living in that city's suburbs. Vern was giving instruction in the game he loved, and the Swedes were admiring Jean.

Vern said, "I guess it actually was put in motion during the 1957 season when we played a Sunday afternoon televised game. Lindsay Nelson was doing that Game of the Week and interviewed me at halftime. It was a normal interview until right at the end. Lindsay knew that I had studied that one summer (1952) at the University of Oslo. He also knew that I spoke Danish, so he asked me to greet my parents in that language. I did just that and the interview signed off.

"It turned out that this guy from the State Department had been watching. He figured that the Danish, Norwegian, and Swedish languages were pretty much alike and that therefore I might be a good candidate for this kind of a trip. Thus the call and our acceptance."

The Mikkelsens spent several weeks as Vern handled the coaching aspect of the assignment, then traveled throughout Sweden as he gave clinics at high schools, YMCAs, and the like. Vern and Jean journeyed "as far north as Kiruna, a mining town above the Arctic Circle in Lapland. We spent the last of the four months traveling around Europe in a rental car and visited relatives in Denmark."

This time the Travelin' Man did not have a precarious seat on a motorcycle. The company was more attractive, too. Through Germany and Austria down to Venice, Italy, went the two vacationing Minnesotans. "Up to Lake Como, then Switzerland and onward to Paris before heading to Copenhagen," Mik explained, sounding more like a travel agent than a professional basketball legend. "There we boarded the ship *Kungsholm*, a brand-new liner. They'd lost my tickets so gave us Super First Class as replacements. Fantastic accommodations on the ten-day trip to New York. Jean made a big hit with some more Scandinavians."

The Swedes, who love their soccer and only abided basketball, saw a triple benefit to Vern's visit—it helped their players get better, showed youngsters the values the game offered, and helped coaches learn how best to instruct their charges. Mikkelsen summed up the trip in a way Coach Kundla must have loved: "It's hard for them to learn our style of tough defense." He added, in his own NBA vernacular: "They have several good players but lack experienced big men."

Ake Nilsson, then president of the Swedish Basketball Association, said Mikkelsen's visit encouraged 16 teams to join the association. In addition to his basketball endeavor, Mikkelsen lectured in English at the Central Institute of Gymnastics, where Princess Birgitta of Sweden's royal family attended.

Mikkelsen, Howie Schultz, Rollie Seltz, Swede Carlson, Tony Jaros, Bud Grant, Whitey Skoog, Dick Garmaker, Chuck Mencel, Joe Hutton Jr., and others represented the unusual tendency in the early days of professional basketball for Upper Midwest athletes to excel.

Arnie Johnson is another case in point. He's a native of Gonvick, Minnesota (home also to pro wrestler Cliff Gustafson of the 1940s in Minneapolis Auditorium fame). Arnie, another Iron Range big boy at 6-5 and 240 pounds, played at Bemidji State and then seven years in the pros with the Royals of Rochester.

"He often squared off against me and they were some bruising battles," Vern said. "One night in the Auditorium I remember in particular, because it is typical of the hard competition yet friendly atmosphere that prevailed with most players in those days. We were warming up and Arnie kind of sidled up to me at midcourt. He said, 'Mik, I want to warn you that tonight you better not be too rough on me. My brothers are here.' I looked up into the stands where he was pointing and there were these three huge guys, wearing almost identical Pendleton shirts and looking for all the world like Paul Bunyan must have. I turned to him with a grin and said something like, 'Hey, I'll take all four of you on.' Or something like that, in my end of what I was sure glad was a joke."

In his seven years, Johnson, another quiet but efficient Minnesotan, averaged nine points a game for 461 Rochester games including playoffs. He was also a very productive rebounder, although exact figures in that category are unavailable because they were not regularly kept until the 1950s.

10

Elgin Baylor Takes a Stand

It is an exciting occasion when a person entering retirement can look back on a final year of accomplishment and say without reservation that it was the best year ever.

In Vern Mikkelsen's case, that is what happened.

The numbers tell a lot, but not everything, about the concluding months of the Askov preacher's kid's ten-year career with the Lakers. Coach Kundla, also in his final year of coaching the team, guided Minneapolis to a stunning finals playoff berth. Mikkelsen, the five-year captain, had his way against almost all the other power forwards in the NBA. It had become commonplace in the position he created to use players even taller and heavier than the 6-foot-7, 235-pound Vern. But the adjective "rugged" was his private domain. Nobody pushed the Hamline grad around, as may be suggested by Mikkelsen's fourteen-point scoring average (second on the 1958-59 team only to rookie Elgin Baylor's twenty-five), his rebounding average of just under ten per game, and his team-leading 81 percent average at the free throw line. All the while, he was extending his amazing Ironman record of consecutive starts, including playoffs, until it eventually reached 715 straight games.

And during that final season Mik also saw his friend Elgin stand tall for a cause.

It was quite a finale by any standards.

"But most of all, I'm pleased with how the team did in

Elgin Baylor

my final season," he said. "From a miserable 19-53 record in 1957-58, last by far in the league, and two sub-par seasons before that, we bounced back to make the playoffs. We beat the Western Division champion St. Louis Hawks in the division playoff finals before losing to Boston in the championship series."

Much of the credit for that remarkable final season in Minnesota goes to Vern's newest teammate, Elgin Baylor, the Seattle University whiz who opted for the NBA prior to his senior season. That decision was made possible because Elgin had first attended the College of Idaho before transferring to Seattle, and his class had graduated, which made him eligible for entry into the NBA.

Vern later talked of Elgin's entry into the league: "He was drafted by us in the spring of 1958. As the 1958-59 season began the following fall, he was extremely reserved, and two of the veterans on the team really gave him a bad time. Elgin had a nervous tick in his left eye and these two vets used to ask him as he was preparing to shoot a free throw if he was checking to see if he'd gotten his Navy stripes yet (in reference to the fact that Elg had been in the service before joining us). I didn't care for their teasing, and God knows the young rookie wasn't happy with it. Coach Kundla asked me to work with Elg to help him break this nervous physical habit, but he could not overcome it.

"Those stripes played an interesting part in one of our last games with St. Louis—or in the retelling of that game, anyway. There were about thirty seconds left in the game, and we were a point behind. Kundla had us call time out to set up a play. Larry Foust, whose shot beat us in the famous Fort Wayne 'stall' game, had since then joined the Lakers, and he thought Coach was going to set something up for

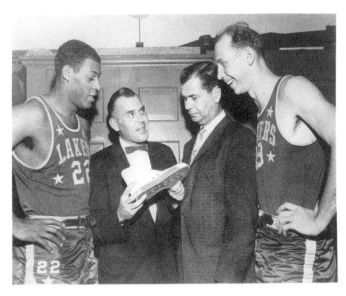

Coach Kundla along with his stars Elgin Baylor and Vern Mikkelsen of the Western Division Champion Minneapolis Lakers look at the new US Royal Basketball shoe they and their teammates helped develop and test.

the two of us. But no, he picked Elgin. Foust and I were disappointed, but of course we did what the coach said. Ed Macauley was guarding Elgin, but he went right around him to score the winning hoop.

"In the locker room after the game, Kundla wanted to make a little hay on his call and asked Elgin to describe what happened. That's when we all saw Elgin break out of his shell for the first time. He boldly grabbed a chair, stood on it, and looking over us all, gave us the following story: 'I got the ball and Macauley was guarding me closely. I checked my stripes, and he must have checked them too, cuz I went right around him for the deuce.' Well, we all laughed heartily and it broke some unspoken tension among the players. It also quieted down those two wily veterans, and from that point on Elgin steadily grew. Unbelievable things were going to happen for Elg, including a chance to speak out in his own way against racism. The Lakers then moved to Los Angeles with Elgin, and Jerry West joined the team. The rest is history.

"People have asked me if John [Kundla] asked me to help teach Elgin the game. Attempting to teach Elgin Baylor anything about the game of basketball would be like teaching Picasso how to paint."

The End of an Era

In their final years in Minneapolis, the crowds arriving to watch the Lakers got smaller and smaller. "Lots of folks had offered their reasons why," Vern said. "But here's what I believe happened in a nutshell. We were gradually running out of places to play. The Auditorium was booking other things like sporting goods, hardware, and auto shows. The St. Paul Auditorium seemed to be out of the loop for Minneapolis ticket buyers. And the Armory was simply too small.

"People were confused as to our game sites. For example, one time when we were set to play a game we were sitting in the locker room at the Armory getting ready to go out and warm up. Elg was not there. We feared that something had happened to him. At the last possible minute, he raced into the locker room. He said, 'I thought we were playing at the Auditorium.' I figured that if even Elg didn't know where we were playing, how could the fans?"

Owner Bob Short, of course, true to his ambitious personality, was trying almost anything to attract fans to Laker games, and that included scheduling "home" games any place in America. One of his attempts to excite fans (and sell tickets) occurred at the Armory, which was about a mile north of the Auditorium in downtown Minneapolis. Vern remembers, "Once, before our last season in Minneapolis, he brought in the Celtics and Philadelphia for an exhibition game at the Armory. He painted the seats different colors depending on their relative location to the court and charged accordingly. Some of the prices, I thought, were a little high for the times. It was the first confrontation of Bill Russell and Wilt Chamberlain, and I was interested enough to go. The place was not filled. Short had even arranged to have one-time Swedish heavyweight champion Ingemar Johannson appear at halftime in a shadow-boxing exhibition in his trunks. It all was a little sad, really, but Short was trying to lure Scandinavians to come even if they didn't care about the basketball. Short was a remarkable man, but not everything he tried worked. When he took our home games around the country, he was giving away what advantage we might have had through familiarity with our surroundings."

"Home" turned out to be places like Winnipeg, Kansas City, New Orleans, Seattle, Buffalo, and Louisville.

"Bob did not care about home court, and you really couldn't blame him. He was desperate. He wasn't the only one using unusual means. Philly, for example, was giving away cheesecakes to take home at the Warrior games. Other towns tried various giveaways, too. But it was the game of basketball, as it was played by professionals, that should have been enough to draw crowds. It was in some places. Boston, for instance. I remember one Easter Sunday in Boston, I attended a service at a Lutheran church. There was an elderly lady sitting near me who recognized me. She was a big Celtics fan and almost was to the scolding stage as to whether I was seeking additional help from God to help beat her Celtics. Some fans were true blue," Mikkelsen said.

For the road warriors of the 1958-59 Laker season, there was one particular trip that bothered Mik well into this century. The Lakers were in Houston once to play Cincinnati and Vern scored forty-three points off Jack Twyman. "My understanding was that cities would give Bob Short a $10,000 fee if we played there. I thought I was scoring just to sell tickets.

"Houston brought us close to Danevang, Texas, fifty miles south of Houston, where my mother's relatives were cotton farmers. She, in fact, was born there in the year 1900 during what has been called the most wicked hurricane and flood in that region's history before Katrina. Those NBA trips, some have said, paved the way for expansion into various communities. I don't know about that, but I remember our difficulties some places with housing. And Elgin's reaction to a particularly ugly situation.

"Some of my relatives had seen me play in Houston against Cincy when I had my best scoring night as a pro with forty-three points. My uncle Verner, who had not previously seen a basketball game, thought that was how I always played. When my cousins and uncles and I went out to dinner after that game, I had to explain to them that it wasn't always that noteworthy.

Mikkelsen being congratulated in the locker room after his career high forty-three points

"Our trip to Houston offered a chance to learn more about some Americans of that era. A day or two earlier, at Charlotte, North Carolina, Bob Short had us quartered at a nice motel. They said we could all stay there except Elgin, Ed Fleming, and Alex "Boo" Ellis because they were black. Kundla told the guy that if they couldn't stay there then we would all leave. The innkeeper didn't budge, so we left. Elgin told us that if they wouldn't let him stay with us, then he would not play. As it was, Elgin didn't play, feeling it was the right thing to do to take a stand no matter what the consequences. I did not know all the details, but Elg was a friend and I stand with my friends.

"Back to our situation in Minneapolis. Without ticket income, how could we exist? Of course, we already had heard that a move to the West Coast was in the works. Truth-

Jean cheering her husband on

fully, we simply were left without a suitable place to play. I had been getting tired of it, especially the constant traveling. My son Tom was not yet a year old when I finally decided this would be it. I had made up my mind that I would some day quit on my own terms. I didn't want to get shoved off the bench. And I wasn't. I simply did not

care to be on the road all the while Tom was growing up. As an aside, Bob offered me 25 percent of the team if I would go to Los Angeles with them. I talked it over with Johnny [Kundla] and we both kind of figured that basketball would not have much of a chance there. For years after, at a Sunday morning breakfast, say, when Jean and I would both be reading the Sunday paper, she would ask, usually from behind a page of the paper, 'Vern, I wonder what that piece of the Lakers would be worth now?' Naturally, I had no appropriate answer."

Years later, Mikkelsen was asked by state legislators to give his opinion on the importance of getting the Target Center built for the Timberwolves. "I spoke to the question by citing our difficulties twenty-five years earlier with no place to play. I told them how badly I thought the city needed it. In fact, the construction of it barely received approval."

Jump back again in time to the period from 1954 to 1958. Pollard and Mikan had retired, and the preternatural power forward was the lone member left of the Three Men of Steel. Still, in 1958-59, the mystique of this prototype power forward, bolstered by the dazzling play of the NBA Rookie-of-the-Year sensation Baylor, continued to pack 'em in on the road—anywhere.

"We played the Celtics once in the Cow Palace in San Francisco in what was our 'home' game. I got to play against Bill Russell and did pretty well. He came into our locker room after the game and asked to talk to me. I was also very pleased that he wanted me to go into the hall outside the locker room to meet his folks and other relatives. Some marvelous relationships existed well after all of us were through playing."

Vern's playing time with the Lakers came to an end in the spring of 1959, "with me walking away knowing I could still help with my play, and I could have. But I did not want to leave Minnesota." In ten seasons Vern played in 699 games, averaging 8½ rebounds and 14½ points a game. He played in six NBA All-Star Games. In 1951, '52, '53, and '54 he was picked to the all-NBA second team. Observers of the pro game back then said, however, the only reason he wasn't first team was because his two mates on the fabulous front line,

Mikan and Pollard, were automatic and deserving choices each year. A third Laker selection was improbable.

That team's second-place finish to Boston in Vern's final year inspired writer Frances Cooper Thompson of Edina, Minnesota, to pen the following:

WHO'S THE WINNER?

There's plenty of praise for the fellow that wins,
And the one who is always the lead.
But little is said for the one left behind,
Who tried but didn't succeed.

Not for him the acclaim
Though his efforts the same,
And his courage equally great.

He ran a good race,
But somehow the pace
Made him only a second too late.

He tries once again . . . his courage still high
Running steadily, always the same
This race, all through life, in peace and strife,
Makes a winner in spite of the name.

With Pollard and Mikan gone, Laker fortunes were not so golden, but Mikkelsen remained the same strong player. He had not had a losing season, high school, college or pro, until 1955-56, but he put it together for one final campaign in 1958-59. Yes, a winner indeed.

11

New Teams, New League

Ten beautiful years, to use Mikkelsen's description of his career with the Lakers, had sped past. It seemed like prehistoric times when the *Minneapolis Star* headline read in the summer of 1949: "Mikkelsen 'Probably' Will Join Lakers." A decade had elapsed since Max Winter signed him and slipped a $100 bill into his dad's coat pocket. Yes, ten years since his muscular play in early Laker scrimmages had some of his teammates kidding him about being an ex-discus thrower (which he was, with records and championships, while at Hamline). Twenty years had elapsed since that seventh-grader wandered into the gym at Askov High (now East Central Junior High) and got his first look at a basketball. Yes, a long time, "but in some ways it felt like yesterday," Vern said.

A ten-year Hall of Fame career, matched by precious few other pro basketball players.

So where did the Askov-Hamline-Laker record-breaker go from here? Well, Mik still had some basketball in his future, even though it didn't require pulling on a uniform, breaking sweat, and showering with the guys.

The success of the nascent American Football League, which eventually succeeded in merging some of its teams into the National Football League, had given basketball promoters and enthusiasts pause for thought, among them a Los Angeles opportunist named Dennis Murphy. He organized a group of twelve investors, receiving $20,000 from each of them. Then he had them draw numbers for franchises in what eventually became the American Basketball Association. George Mikan was named commissioner and opened an office in the Farmers & Merchants Bank in Minneapolis. The first season was in 1967. Larry Shields had the Minneapolis franchise, calling the team the Muskies. Jim Pollard was hired as coach. Mikkelsen eventually became general manager during the first season, succeeding Eddie Hollman. It had been eight years since the Lakers departed for Los Angeles.

At the two-thirds mark of the 1967 season, Shields advised Mikkelsen that the team was moving immediately to Miami and that all employees should report there the following Monday. Vern said, "The only reason I took the job in the first place was that it was in Minnesota. I told Shields that I certainly was not going. Period." Pollard, however, went to Miami as coach of what was then going to be known as the Floridians. Vern said, "I went back to the insurance business I had entered when I left the playing floor, happy to live where I was."

Soon, though, another challenge loomed. The Pittsburgh Pipers of the ABA decided to move to Minneapolis in a desperate search of a more lucrative venue.

Vern said, "With what was to be called the Pipers in Minneapolis also, I was offered the same job that I had with the Muskies. It looked appealing, especially because they had a super-star in Connie Hawkins. I jumped at the chance to be their general manager. However, things declined dramatically at mid-season when The Hawk injured a knee. Recovery took almost to the end of the season. I even did some scrimmaging with him at the St. Thomas gym to get him ready for the end of the season. The knee finally was OK, but, of course, he had not been playing at all in games. As we hammered on each other in scrimmaging, we became good friends. But he was not able to return to playing form before the season ended.

Mikkelsen as Minnesota Pipers' General Manager and interim coach, 1969

"While all of this was taking place, a decision had been made back in California by Dennis Murphy to build his own team around The Hawk the following season. It never happened, however, because The Hawk settled his differences with the NBA—a suspension because of alleged but never proven gambling charges. He won his suit and moved into stardom in the NBA, eventually going into the Hall of Fame. Not bad for a playground kid from New York City. He had been the MVP of the 1968 season for Pittsburgh, then called the Rens. He was an all-star again the next ABA season with the Pipers, after the team moved to Minneapolis. He also traveled a bit with the Globetrotters during those years. He finished with seven seasons in the NBA, playing for the Suns, the Lakers in L.A., and Atlanta, then went into public relations with the Suns."

During the 1968-69 term of Mikkelsen's tenure as general manager of Minneapolis in the ABA, a dramatic and unusual coaching situation developed. Jim Harding was coach of the Pipers after Jim Pollard left with the Muskies to Miami. As a result of the team's on-court success during the 1967-68 season under Pollard, Harding had inherited the right to coach the West in the 1969 ABA All-Star Game in Louisville. At a dinner party the night before the game, Harding and Gabe Rubin, the principal owner of the Pipers, got into a scuffle for some unknown reason. The fight, which Vern helped to break up, occurred at the height of the banquet. Vern said, "It was a sad deal all the way around. Both ended up rumpled and at least a little embarrassed. George, as the commissioner, heard about the fight and fired Harding on the spot. Then he asked me to coach the West in the game. And to coach the Pipers thereafter. I said that I would coach them only until another coach could be found.

"I had become a good friend of Gus Young. He coached at Gustavus Adolphus, where we had done some of our Laker pre-season workouts, and we had been wonderfully fed by Evelyn Young, Gus's wife, who headed food service there. I knew Evelyn did not want Gus to coach any more, but after two and a half weeks I had done quite enough coaching and Gus wanted to take over. He did so for the remainder of the season even though Evelyn wasn't very happy with the idea."

The next year, the Pipers moved back to Pittsburgh. There, and elsewhere, the ABA owners hoped to secure franchises in the NBA. "About fifteen of those owners lost out," Mikkelsen said. "Indianapolis, Denver, San Antonio, and the New York Nets got in. The Pipers of 1968-69 actually made the ABA playoffs under Gus, but lost in the first round to the Floridians in Miami.

"Gus? He wound up with a very popular bowling alley along Highway 100 in the western suburbs of Minneapolis."

Mikan and Mikkelsen took pride in one ABA legacy— the three-point field goal. It slowly made its way into college and high school ball and has altered the way the closing minutes of many a game are played. "No play can change a game as quickly as a three-pointer," Elgin Baylor said. Another innovation of the ABA didn't fare so well—the multi-colored ball. One ABA novelty, probably used only in Minneapolis, came after Shields decided something should be done to highlight the moment "when a three-point shot went in for us," Mik said. Dick Jonckowski, public-address announcer for the Muskies-Pipers, was told to find some kind of a horn to blow on those occasions. Vern said, "He found a real, real loud one. When Connie was at the scorer's table to check in for us for the first time, a three-pointer went in for us and Jonckowski blew the horn. The Hawk almost jumped out of his skin."

Those ABA games were played at the Metropolitan Sports Center in Bloomington, which was built after the Lakers' departure in 1960. For nicknames out of the past to ponder when remembering the ABA, try these: the Americans of New Jersey, the Colonels of Kentucky, the Amigos of Anaheim, the Mavericks of Houston, the Buccaneers of New Orleans, the Oaks of Oakland, the Chaparrals of Dallas, the Rockets of Denver and, of course, the Pipers and Muskies. Mel Daniels, out of the University of New Mexico, averaged 22 points for the Muskies one season, passing up a Cincinnati NBA offer to play in the ABA for a $24,000 salary and a $14,000 bonus. After only one season, financially strapped co-owner Larry Shields sold Daniels' contract for $15,000 to the Indiana's Pacers.

Mikkelsen remembered, "Things began to unravel gradually. We had a good team and a good organization. But when Mel left for Indiana, the handwriting was on the wall. They tried to sell some stock locally, but it didn't fly. So the team did—to Miami. With the Pipers, there was The Hawk to make us go, and for me to stay with it as general manager. But Harding pushed the players way too hard, for one thing, and we couldn't draw the kind of fan numbers that encourage good play." Mikan's memories late in his life were "how hard we worked to make the ABA go. We just couldn't get stability at the ownership level."

12

Reminiscences:
Coaches and Friends

In many ways, Arild Verner Agerskov Mikkelsen grew up like an only child. His third name was thrown in there because it was the Denmark home town of his maternal grandpa Jens Peter Agerskov Petersen. Vern was close to but actually lived far away from much of his extended family.

Sisters Esther and Hertha were six and four years older, respectively, and gone from home by the time Vern became a standout on the Askov High School athletic scene as a sophomore. Esther attended St. Olaf for a time, then studied to become a medical technician in Duluth. (She died of cancer in 1992.) Hertha went to business college, then was off to Washington, D.C., where she met Joe Jackson. They were married in Houston. They moved back to Minneapolis and a brother-sister relationship resumed. Vern was busy, but they had Laker tickets. Joe was best man at Jean and Vern's wedding. Hertha assisted with the coffee serving at the reception. She died in 2002, the same year as Vern's wife Jean.

Of his two basketball coaches after high school, Hamline's Joe Hutton seemed to Mik like a "second father/advisor" and John Kundla "like a brother."

In high school, Vern's closest friend was Folmer Frederiksen, a classmate and the smartest kid in their grade. He died after being shot while deer hunting near the family farm outside Askov in 1945. Vern said, "I still remember him as a faithful pal."

His friend Folmer's death provided Vern with the first tragedy that was accompanied by a feeling of "this shouldn't have happened!" Vern remembers being on the practice court at Hamline the first fall he was away from home. "I was called to the telephone by someone who said my dad had to talk to me. Just by that, I knew it had to be something serious. A lot of things were running through my mind as I hurried to the phone, family things. Then he told me what had happened to Folmer, who was the one among us Askov kids of whom the most was expected. College, then we knew not what, something governmental we were sure, with the brains that Folmer had shown us throughout high school.

"He was from a large farm family, and he and his brothers had hunted since they were old enough to use a rifle safely. They were all very familiar with the area they were hunting in. They wounded a deer but it ran off. They knew it was hiding in a particular grove of trees, and decided to surround it and force it out. Somehow a rifle was fired; and later the word was that more than one of them shot at the deer as it scrambled from one bit of underbrush to another. A bullet found Folmer and killed him. A terrible mistake had occurred that the brothers dreaded thinking about for years after."

At Hamline, Vern's best friend was Fish Leiviska, a Finn from Virginia, Minnesota. They were Norton Fieldhouse roommates for three years and as such shared many thoughts and experiences.

Yet Vern was a boy, later a man, who often kept to himself. He had lots of friends, but his interests took in him a
myriad of directions. Lest it be forgotten, however, he persis-
tently credited "three elements—family, friends, and faith—
for whatever I have accomplished."

As Vern looks back on his storied life, his first awareness
of day-to-day developments outside Askov came during the
early years of World War II. "We had blackouts which were
supervised by air-raid warden Ancher Simonsen, who was
the town constable." Vern's father, as the Danish Lutheran
pastor, was looked to by most of the 350 inhabitants of the
community as a person to follow and listen to, "and Dad
toed the line," Vern said. "We followed to the letter all the
blackout rules. Dad was especially concerned for us because
of the proximity of the Mesabi Iron Range and what it meant
to our country's war effort. I heard adults talking about what
the Nazis were doing to Jews, a treatment I just could not
comprehend. We had lots of relatives in occupied Denmark
and my parents and others watched carefully what King
Christian was doing." King Christian X ruled Denmark from
1912 to 1947. He imposed World War II seclusion upon
himself in a manner that Danes, and many others worldwide, accepted as symbolic of a quiet national resistance to
the occupation by Germany. "My parents were proud of their
heritage. That was instilled early and easily in me."

There is an inescapable conclusion to be drawn in Vern's
life, just as ethnicity can be seen to recede through genera-
tions in other nationalities. A traditional Danish food such as
smörrebröd (open-face sandwiches made with rye bread and
topped with either minced meat or herring) did not appeal
to him. "I much preferred what Mom made seems like every

Monday," Vern said. "She had a special skillet with rounded indentations on the bottom and used something like pancake dough to make aebleskiver. I could hardly get enough of those doughnut-like delights. Yes, I was Danish and appreciated that. But not to the exclusion of respecting other people's beliefs, or to do something, like eat smörrebröd, just because it was Danish to do it. You could give me, for instance, a hamburger any time."

From his parents, Vern inherited his life-long attitude of compassion for others. "My dad used to say that you can most easily be treated with respect if you show the same to others."

An example of this selfless attitude is Vern's relationship with David L. Valen, a retired pastor from Vern's Minnetonka neighborhood. Pastor Valen said, "I grew up in Butterfield, Minnesota, where my dad [Elmer] was a Lutheran pastor serving Butterfield and [neighboring] Odin. I spent many an evening listening to Laker games on the radio. Vern's autographed picture hung in my room. I was moved to write a letter to a Laker. I could have written to any one of them. I knew them all by what I had read, their wives' names, where they went to school, where they grew up, all things like that. But it was Vern who was my favorite, my hero actually, so my letter went to him.

"You can imagine my surprise when I received a three-page hand-written answer from him. My family kept it in a scrapbook through the years. One day, I believe it was in 1984, I was visiting a member of Westwood Lutheran, where I was pastor, at St. Louis Park's Methodist Hospital. In the hospital I heard this giant of a man ask a nurse where he could find 'Mrs. Hutton.' I knew that was the name of the Hamline coach, figured it was his wife the man was asking about, and blurted out, 'Excuse me, but are you Vern Mikkelsen?' Of course it was, and I told him about our exchange of letters some thirty or so years earlier, and how much his letter had meant to me. Well, he seemed interested but cautious. He said he'd like to see the letters, and he did so one day in my office. I invited him to our church in St. Louis Park some Sunday when he could make it. It was Palm Sunday when he showed up. I was to talk about the heroic aspect of Jesus and the values of love and kindness that Jesus demonstrated.

"I told the congregation that I had a particular hero of my own when I was a young man, and that he was right here in a front pew. I asked Vern to come up, and he did. There wasn't much of a recognition factor with the kids. But their parents and grandparents sure knew who Vern was. What he shared with them was priceless, the value of teamwork, the importance of kindness. The kids were spellbound."

Valen, 100 percent Norwegian, had been moved to write Mikkelsen because they were both minister's sons, both Boy Scouts, both newspaper carriers. He said that he was impressed by Vern's sincerity as he spoke to the kids. "He said they should notice that after a basket, as a team returns to the defensive end, the guy who scores usually points a finger at the player whose assist made it possible. He said that was to acknowledge the fact that no one can score all alone."

"Always remember the value of teamwork," was what Valen recalled as Mikkelsen's advice on that Palm Sunday. "Life's like that. We all benefit when we help one another."

Of Valen, Vern said, "Quite simply, he is just a great person."

Mikkelsen, understandably, was an athletic hero in Danish outposts in South Dakota, Montana, Wisconsin, Minnesota, Iowa, Nebraska, and California. But, because of his association with Valen and others like him, his popularity swelled across a broad ethnic and religious landscape.

There is no better way to view that aspect of Mikkelsen's life than through his fifty-year friendship with John Kundla. "I have always felt that John was like the brother I never had," Vern said.

When Mikkelsen became a Laker in late summer of 1949 at age twenty, Kundla was an extremely youthful yet "veteran" coach.

Kundla, thirty-three at the time they met, was willing to lend a sympathetic and thoughtful ear whenever Mikkelsen needed one. They discussed life, basketball, and the importance of a strong belief in God—Kundla, the devout Catholic, and Mikkelsen, the devout Lutheran.

"I could talk to John about anything," Vern said. "Not only that, we thought alike on so many things. I knew that he could understand my passion about events that occurred in my life, things that others might have thought to be quite trivial. Once we were discussing the life of a hobo on the road, hitching rides on trains, going no place in particular —in both the actual and the philosophical sense. I told John that in Askov, with the train tracks so near our house, hobos would continually come around looking for a meal. Mom never turned one down. But they had to eat on the porch, not inside. John indicated that he thought he understood what my mom was all about, just from that bit of information."

Kundla is one of only a dozen men who have coached an NBA champion in their first season with a franchise.

In Kundla's case, that was in 1949, the year before Mikkelsen arrived. In actuality, he had coached the Lakers to a title in the National Basketball League the previous year, too, but the NBA does not recognize the 1948 championship. Rather, the league recognized the Baltimore Bullets as champion that year. The Bullets won the crown in the Basketball Association of America, which played only a 48-game regular season. But NBA historians picked the Bullets to be listed as 1947-48 NBA champs because the BAA played in larger cities with bigger arenas than those in the NBL. As far as which team was better, the Lakers or the Bullets, the Lakers moved into the BAA the following season and proved a point. They won the 1949 championship. The Bullets, overshadowed by both the Lakers and another newcomer from the NBL, Rochester, failed to play even .500 ball.

What all those statistical findings amount to, simply put, is this: Whenever the professional basketball titles won by the Lakers while stationed in Minneapolis are listed, simply add the one with the National Basketball League in 1947-48, which would make it six, even though five is the accepted number. And all the titles came with Kundla as coach.

When Vern was first exposed to the coaching of Kundla in 1949 (after the contract-signing that his dad had to do because Vern was not yet 21), Mikkelsen found what he had expected. "I had heard that John was exactly like what I had been used to in college with Coach Hutton—demanding but fair."

The two hit it off from the start.

In fact, if there is merit in the belief that skill stands still unless there is a loving push, it is thrice evident here. Vern's adult "pushes" came from Coach Hutton, wife Jean, and John Kundla.

Vern, the small-town kid with the small-college background, looked at Kundla as surprisingly "old school" for what the newest Laker had expected to be a pretty urbane big-city guy.

After all, Kundla was born on the day before the Fourth of July in 1916. Nine months later the United States declared war on Germany in World War I. Star Junction, Pennsylvania, Kundla's birthplace, is only twenty miles southeast of Pittsburgh, almost a suburb. Kundla grew up though, in Minneapolis, starring in sports at Central High. He played at the University of Minnesota and helped the Gophers to the Big Ten basketball crown as a sophomore in 1937. His coach at Minnesota was Dave MacMillan, who in the early 1950s assisted Kundla in coaching the Lakers. Kundla also played baseball well enough to give organized baseball a try for one year. In 1939 he played Class C baseball for Paducah, Kentucky.

In 1943 and 1944 Kundla played basketball with a semi-pro team out of Shakopee, Minnesota, along with several former Gophers whom he would later coach during the Lakers' inaugural season. They were Warren Ajax, Don Smith, Ken Exel, and Tony Jaros.

Kundla coached the Lakers for twelve seasons in all, with 466-319 and 70-38 records for regular season and playoffs, respectively. His teams missed league playoffs only in the 1957-58 campaign, when some two dozen games were played on neutral courts. Mikkelsen played his entire career under Kundla as coach, although George Mikan coached some games in 1957-58, and John Castellani in 1958-59. (Castellani had been Elgin Baylor's coach at Seattle.)

Mikan pouring coffee for Mikkelsen and Kundla at Mickey's Diner, 1989

Fittingly, Mikkelsen and Kundla went into the Basketball Hall of Fame the same year, 1995. Mikan was a charter member (1959) of the Hall. Pollard went in in 1978 and Slater Martin in 1982. Mikkelsen's career-high season scoring average was just a shade less than 19 points a game in 1954-55, the year after Mikan retired. That team lost in the Western Division playoff finals.

The little things remained dear to Kundla. "I was a referee for the Oshkosh-Sheboygan exhibition in Minneapolis December 1, 1946," he said. "Early on with the Lakers, I did everything, including the ankle taping. I remember how it used to bother me when people claimed that all we did was walk the ball up the floor and feed it to George. We always looked for the fast break first. With our rebounding, we got it plenty."

There was conjecture that Mikkelsen and Kundla might have been disappointed not to be inducted into the Hall of Fame sooner than they were. "That's not so at all," Vern said. "It could not have been better. For us, going in together was the big thing. We were both delighted that it worked out that way. For those who went into the Hall the first year of eligibility, they did so with children sometimes too young to enjoy it. With me, and John, too, it was better because our kids, in my case Tom and John, were old enough to appreciate what was taking place. They thoroughly enjoyed sharing the experience with me and Jean and John and his wife Marie and their six children."

Marie was a particularly good friend of Jean, as was Pat Mikan. "Marie and Jean were part and parcel of the whole Kundla-Mikkelsen deal," Vern said in 2005, during George Mikan's final days of life. "We did an awful lot of things together, continuing long after our days with the Lakers. Yep, John, to this day seems like a brother."

The feeling is mutual. Kundla said, "The thrill of going into the Hall of Fame in 1995 was made even more so because we went in together. I have been fortunate all my life, in marrying Marie, in my family, and in having a friend like Mik. In addition, how could any coach be so lucky as to have on his team the greatest front line in the game's history?

"Going into the Hall with Vern was almost like three of us being honored. Because without George Mikan none of those things would have happened to any of us. He made it all possible." Mikan always credited DePaul coach Ray Meyer with making him a player. So it's understandable that Kundla picked Meyer as his presenter for the Hall induction at Springfield. Bob Pettit presented Mikkelsen in the ceremony.

"I had total respect for Bob, as a player and as an individual," Vern said. "As we walked to the podium, I thought, 'This is the longest I've been around him that he didn't score on me.' He was an automatic choice."

Kundla recalls giving up professional coaching to stay at Minnesota and coach the Gophers, even though he was asked by Bob Short to go with the team to Los Angeles. "Vern and I agreed," Kundla said. "We just wanted to stay in Minnesota. By then travel wasn't nearly so bad because we flew everywhere. But being with my family more was the deciding thing."

Kundla remembers three basketball trips outside pro ball that he enjoyed immensely. "When I was playing AAU ball with the Rock Springs Sparklers in Shakopee, one of quite a few exceptional AAU clubs in Minnesota, we went to Chicago for one tournament and to Denver for another. These were national tournaments with teams and players from all over America. We even played the Globetrotters."

In 1964, five years after leaving the Lakers, Kundla coached the U.S. team to the championship in the World University Games in Budapest, Hungary. "I'll never forget the thrill of seeing our flag go up to the top," he said. "But part of the enjoyment of that particular tournament was coaching wonderful young men like Bill Bradley and Tom and Dick Van Arsdale."

Much of the joy in parenting and grandparenting is having an opportunity to share with someone interested the accomplishments of the offspring. For grandfather John Kundla, Mikkelsen was the perfect partner in such discussions. Kundla learned of "sensational" doings by Vern's two young grandsons in Phoenix. That gave Kundla a chance to talk about something extremely dear to his heart: "My grand-kids playing basketball, and playing it well, offers them the same type of making true friends and creating memories that Vern and I had. It all started when my daughter Kathleen took a teaching job in Ely, Minnesota. There she met Nate Dahlman. He had played basketball at Gustavus. After they married they decided to raise their family near but not in the Twin Cities. They picked Braham, a town of 1,200 people about 65 miles north of St. Paul."

Braham may not have been very well known when Nate and Kathleen moved there, but that has changed decidedly in recent years, as major-college basketball recruiters by the dozens visited the school to take a look at Kundla's grandson Isaiah Dahlman, a senior in the fall of 2005, and his broth-er Noah, one year younger. Braham was ranked in the top twenty nationally in 2005 among boys' high school teams by *USA TODAY*, in the top five in the Midwest. The team again was ranked nationally in 2006. The gyms were packed by late afternoon both at home and on the road when the Bombers had a game scheduled.

Six-foot-seven point-guard Isaiah Dahlman, who led the Braham Bombers to three straight Class 2A state championships (2004-05-06), was courted by Michigan State, Minnesota, Illinois, Iowa, Stanford, Georgia Tech, Connecticut, UCLA, and Kentucky. He eventually signed with Michigan State. Noah, a 6-6 post player, has similar but not quite the same star-attraction to recruiters as his older brother, who was Minnesota's Mr. Basketball and the *Associated Press* pick for Minnesota Player of the Year in 2006.

"One of the benefits of Isaiah's recognition has been his invitation to play all over against America's best high school players, many of them a year ahead of him in school," Grandpa Kundla said. "He learned just what it takes to make it at a top program, where he had to improve. We pray that Isaiah, and Noah too, make the right decisions in life, including when it comes to a college. But they make up their own minds." Isaiah and Noah both were pass receivers on Braham's football team. "I just prayed they wouldn't get hurt," said Grandpa. "Pray" is the important word in all of this. It is not by accident, but by design, that the younger siblings of Isaiah and Noah are Jonah, Hannah, Rebecca, and Zachariah. "Like my family," Mikkelsen said, "John's family believes in the power of prayer." Brother to brother respect, indeed.

Mikan, incidentally, was not totally unfamiliar with Braham. When talking about Kundla's grandchildren late in the big center's life, he had this recollection: "When I ran for U.S. Congress in 1956 [the campaign was run by Marjorie Shanard] I remember Braham quite well. I was coming home from a meeting there when I fell asleep at the wheel and swerved into a ditch. I thank God nothing more serious happened. It served as a warning for me not to drive alone."

Vern's coach at Hamline, Joe Hutton, died June 13, 1988, nine days before his eighty-ninth birthday. The funeral gave Mikkelsen time to think. It was officiated by Reverend Rick Ireland at Hamline United Methodist Church, and Vern was asked by the Hutton family to say a few words.

"I had done similar things at various venues by that time," Vern later said, "but I was extremely nervous considering the circumstances. The notes I made on the program say it all. First, I was going to recite the Twenty-third Psalm, which I had memorized in childhood and recited many times since. Still, I wrote the words on the program right from 'The

Lord is my shepherd' on through 'dwell in the house of the Lord forever.' Then I made a note to thank Ann Simley, a wonderful Hamline speech and drama instructor who had assisted me in a similar assignment forty years previous at a school chapel. I called my time at the Hutton lectern 'a unique coincidence.'

"And of course I did not need to write down these words, but I did: 'No one person was as responsible for the direction of my life as JWH [Coach Hutton]. It is an honor and a privilege to participate in the memorializing of Joe Hutton.' And I meant every word.

"Before there was talk of present classifications of small and Division One schools and all of that, I was lucky that Coach filled our schedule with teams like DePaul, Stanford, Wyoming, Long Island University, Arizona State, Texas Christian, and many, many more big schools."

Mikkelsen said, "I'm sure I had been to both coasts before most of my peers in Minnesota. We held our own as we went all over to play. That certainly broadened my perspective as to my country. Coach always mixed into our trips interesting side journeys off the court. I think it brought us even more closely together in an extension of his total-team concept." Vern also thought often about how Coach Hutton's background in education played quietly into his own. How Coach had been a Phi Beta Kappa student at Carleton (graduating in 1924). How he had taken his young coaching mind on the road to Sioux Falls, South Dakota, and Hopkins, Minnesota (as well as Northfield, Minnesota, the site of Carleton College) for high school jobs before being hired at Hamline.

Coach Hutton emphasized winning, of course, with a success rate of 76 percent during thirty-four years at

Hamline, but never forgot to stress that it was only through devotion to learning the fundamentals of the game that winning came.

People clamored for a game between the University of Minnesota and Hamline's Pipers. But Coach Hutton understood Minnesota coach Ozzie Cowles' difficulty in dealing with such a request—nothing to gain and everything to lose. So when Cowles asked, Hutton brought his team quietly to the Gopher campus to scrimmage. Score was not formally kept, but the upper hand leaned toward Mikkelsen and his teammates.

At least partly because he took Hamline a dozen times to the national small-college tournament of his era, claiming championships in 1942, 1949 with Vern, and 1951, Hutton was immortalized by his school in a significant manner. The Norton Fieldhouse on the Hamline campus was renamed the Joe W. Hutton Fieldhouse in his honor. And, as is far too seldom the case, it was done in 1986, while Hutton was still alive. Coincidentally, Hutton's visitation prior to the memorial service at United Methodist was conducted at Dawn Valley Funeral Home south of Minneapolis. That was a business run at one time by an old Piper foe from Gustavus, Bob Werness.

Congestive heart failure had taken Coach from Vern, but nothing could halt the flood of memories thereafter. "Coach died at Methodist Hospital in St. Louis Park where just a few years earlier I had my wonderful meeting with Reverend Dave [Valen]."

At the funeral of his father, Joe Hutton Jr. said, "I marveled at how in later life those same players I watched him coach became some of Dad's very best friends." Joe Jr. played at Hamline for his father from 1946 to 1950. Another son, Tom, played for the Pipers from 1958 to 1962.

As he sat at his coach's funeral, Mikkelsen realized that the God-driven serendipity that brought him to Hamline in the first place included an unusual basketball education. The coach there, his revered Joe, brought an emphasis of defense over offense, plus futuristic methods of effecting back-door baskets and rolling off screens. He did so considerably before others were doing the same, copying him. "What a great place for me to learn the game, from Coach and Howie Schultz," Vern said.

From the church where Coach Joe was memorialized, Mikkelsen could gaze across the Hamline campus and recall what a bumpkin he had felt himself to be when he arrived. "Being from Askov, which hardly anybody had heard of, I just knew that I was the most peculiar new freshman to show up."

13

Pollard, Mikan, and the Importance of "Family"

Jean and Vern celebrated his being voted into the Basketball Hall of Fame in a luxurious, private way. They cruised the Bahamas.

"Back then," Vern said, "the Norwegian Cruise Line had a special arrangement for NBA players and retirees like myself. It consisted of a free cruise, in our case through the Bahamas. Howie Schultz and his wife Gloria had done it earlier and told us about it.

"I got the news I was going into the Hall in March of 1995. We booked the cruise for April. The boys were adults then, so we could be gone. It was for ten days on the cruise line's flagship, the *Norway*. With the deal they gave, the Norwegian Cruise Line could bill itself as The Official Cruise Line of the NBA. We had a wonderful celebration and could stay as much to ourselves as we wanted to because we had a little patio just for us. They did lots of little things especially for us. All I had asked for that was special was an eight-foot bed. And it was in our room when we went into it."

Throughout his life, Mikkelsen has had an intense sense of family—in some unusual ways.

Mr. and Mrs. J. P. Agerskov Petersen, Vern's maternal grandparents

He said, "Of course there is the normal family, my grandparents, aunts, uncles, parents, sisters, wife, children and so on. But think of the other families that I have had.

"Most certainly, there has been my Hamline family; then, in fact, my medical family, which got me through Jean's difficulties and my own. And of course, my Laker family, primarily George, Jim Pollard, and us three who were rookies together—me, Dugie, and Bob Harrison."

Vern's grandparents on his father's side were somewhat unknown to him, living back in Denmark. His dad and uncle had come to America to work in Tyler, Minnesota, a strong Danish community. His father, believing he was wronged by someone at Tyler, headed off to Grand View College in Des Moines, determined to become a Danish Lutheran pastor. He not only became a pastor in Des Moines, but also met his wife-to-be there. Through thick and thin, mostly thin, he and wife Elna raised two girls and a boy on a meager subsistence that characterized many Danish Lutheran congregations. "At times, it seems we lived on love," Vern said.

In many ways Vern's success in basketball is tied to his faith in family tradition. "An example would be my mom's dad," Vern said. "He took his home town of Agerskov and inserted it in his name between Jens Peter and Petersen. It wasn't just to complicate matters. Rather, it was because he thought Petersen was too common a name to be practical in America.

"That certainly was easy enough for me to understand. As a young boy I realized my full name was a bit complicated, difficult to say, and for some hard to remember. But I admired J.P., as he liked to be called, as a grandpa who excelled. He was an extremely eager reader, something I believe my mom and I inherited. He wrote extensively, especially on issues dealing with religion. Then he winds up in south Texas, near Danevang, to try to make a living in agriculture.

"I can imagine his frustration in those first years in this country. He tried the traditional crops that he knew about from Denmark, but the climate and the soil worked against him. He didn't keep beating his head against a wall. He got into cotton as did so many farmers around him. And he did very, very well at it. Enough so that he could send my mom up to college at Grand View where she met Dad. They married and Dad, with Mom to assist in so many ways, took on his first congregation in Elkhorn, Iowa, where now there is a museum full of memorabilia relating to the Danish movement into this country.

"From Iowa, as has been discussed, there were the family movements to California, then Wisconsin, then Montana, then Askov. By the way, it used to tickle my Hamline and Laker friends when I explained that the town, if you used strictly the Danish approach, would be pronounced 'Osco'— that's right, just like the drug store. At any rate, Askov residents became extensions of family for me, especially after my sisters left home."

An advertisement from a 1959 Lakers program

The Hamline family also became special. "First there was Howie Schultz, who drilled me incessantly on the court, all for my own good, naturally. And also, as it turned out, for the good of Hamline basketball.

"Then there was Fish Leiviska. We roomed together for three years. When I got to Hamline and lived over by Macalester, I told Coach Hutton that I would not be able to afford much in the way of housing, like, say, a fraternity. He said not to worry, and I didn't. Rollie Seltz, who was a senior when I was a freshman, roomed in the fieldhouse with Dick Ryan.

"When they graduated, Coach Hutton told me to move into their room, which I did. Not long after, when I came back to the room after morning classes, there was Leiviska, with a couple of boxes. He told me that Coach had said it was OK for him to join me in the fieldhouse room. We were together three years.

"A word about my relationship with Howie and Rollie is needed here. They were older, and as such, kind of like seasoned college advisors on most any subject. Advice ranged from places to sneak to off campus, to good study routines, and girls. But it was basketball and its importance in the Hamline scheme of things that they emphasized. And how could I not listen? Howie had scored 21 points against DePaul and George in 1944. Rollie scored 24 when we played them my first season."

Mikkelsen talked often of the lifetime relationships developed at Hamline, "like with Rollie, Howie, Coach Hutton, Fish and Joe Jr. For a while after I left the basketball court, while I was getting my feet on the ground in the insurance business, I rented office space from Fish."

Not long after he went into the insurance business, Mikkelsen joined the Minneapolis Chamber of Commerce, and under the leadership of another Hamline alumnus, Norm McGrew, he served a term as chairman of the Chamber's Sports and Attractions committee.

For Vern's 1995 induction into the Hall of Fame, honoring him with their presence at Springfield were Schultz, Seltz, George Dress (a football player friend),

Larry Osness (president of Hamline then), Glenn Gumlia (from the 1942 national champs), niece Jeanne Davis, and nephew Jim Jackson. Arilee Pollard and Bob Harrison hosted a party with many Hall of Famers on hand. Sons John and Tom, and Tom's wife Jennifer, celebrated too, right alongside Vern.

Seltz remembers the Hall of Fame weekend as one where he thought back on his early appraisals of Mikkelsen. "He was a bashful, small-town sixteen-year-old kid, raw, but with huge ambition." Seltz was also a Lutheran minister's son, who had come to Hamline from St. Paul Humboldt, and saw improvement day by day in this youngster who had moved into the center spot under Coach Hutton. A basketball player who knew the game well, Seltz assessed Mikkelsen as raw, but with almost unmatched potential. After his senior year at Hamline, Seltz played for the College All-Stars against Fort Wayne in what at that time (1946) featured the pro champion playing in Chicago against the Stars. There followed four years of professional ball, three of them with Howie Schultz at Anderson, Indiana. Actually, it was four years plus eighteen or so games in 1950-51 with the St. Paul Lights. That marked a brief episode in Twin Cities sports history with Schultz as player-coach, plus Hal Haskins, Seltz, and Ken Mauer as local talent. "The Korean War killed the Lights as much as anything," Seltz said.

In August of 1995, Hamline sponsored a Hall of Fame selection tent party in Mikkelsen's honor. Wife Jean and John Kundla were at Vern's side. He visited and renewed friendships with acquaintances from college days like track teammates Kerwin Engelhart, Dick Klaus and Keith Paisley. "A very nice event," said Mikkelsen.

Vern's Laker Family

Among the fascinating aspects of Vern's basketball career is the way the cast with whom he is most easily identified was assembled. First came Jim Pollard, who had been determined to stick with AAU ball until the 1948 Olympics. However, Laker front-office persistence and the offer of what then was an extremely large pro basketball contract of $12,000 changed his mind. As a result, the brand-new 1947 franchise had its first true star—the soaring "Kangaroo Kid."

In November of that year, after the demise of the Professional Basketball League of America, the Lakers earned the rights to George Mikan in a dispersal draft of PBLA players.

"They were idols of mine," Mikkelsen remembers. "I had watched them while I was a junior and senior at Hamline. And here I was, playing with them. Part of the thrill was that I learned that if I did things the way Coach Kundla told me to, I could hold my own in this league." That was in the early weeks of the 1949-50 season.

Blended into the mixture was the quickness of Slater Martin and the steadiness of Bob Harrison. They had been drafted with Mikkelsen in 1949 but spent their initial season playing behind three-year regular and captain Herman Schaefer and two-season starter Arnie Ferrin. Schaefer retired the next year and Ferrin the year after that. During those four astonishing seasons before Mikan retired in 1954, the Lakers had a cumulative 178-98 regular-season record and won three straight NBA championships (1952-54). Perhaps the most amazing thing was that three of the contributors to those championship seasons had been rookies in 1949-50.

Harrison, Martin, Pollard, Mikan, and Mikkelsen constituted what Vern now refers to as the "Lakers' first family with Kundla." Harrison was traded away in 1954 and Martin in 1956. Pollard retired in 1955. Others filled the four starting spots, of course, but it was never quite the same. The era of the Three Rookies and Two Legends was over.

There were definitely many other expressions of what amounted to family with the Lakers.

One example would be the barnstorming trips the team took over the years to make extra money and spread good will for the franchise. Laker players would venture into the Dakotas, Iowa, Wisconsin, and many Minnesota towns to play games, with the proceeds usually devoted to a worthy local cause, though the players would make a few bucks, too. One situation the barnstormers sometimes found themselves in was a game against a locally-assembled team of basketball players of varying degrees of talent, size, and age. Occasionally, those games would get nasty. Locals might try anything to trip up a pro, "and I mean anything," Mikkelsen said. "But

The barnstorming Laker "family" arrives in Devils Lake, North Dakota, with their fancy hats in 1951. Bud Grant is on the right.

usually they were nothing but good, clean fun." Whenever possible, the Lakers preferred to bring a split squad—one team of Laker stars, and the other of various teammates and friends called the "NBA All-Stars."

Generally, through the early 1950s, Bud Grant, Harrison, Martin, Mikan, Mikkelsen, and Pollard would comprise the Lakers. Most often, Kleggie Hermsen, Joe Hutton Jr., Tony Jaros, Ed Mikan, Kevin O'Shea, and Howie Schultz would be the "All-Stars." All except Hermsen and Ed Mikan had pulled on a Laker jersey several times. Hermsen, 6-9, played at Minnesota. Ed Mikan, 6-8, played at DePaul. Hermsen played eight years of professional ball starting at Sheboygan, Wisconsin in 1943. Ed Mikan, George's younger brother by one and a half years, played six years in the pros ending in Boston in 1954.

"The barnstorming, I think, brought us closer together than we already were," Mikkelsen said. "I remember one trip in particular, into South and North Dakota, when Pat Kennedy, in a class by himself as an NBA referee, traveled with us. I think that was in the spring after my first season. I can remember us rolling into Devils Lake, North Dakota, wearing crazy colored caps that Bob Berger, Ben's son and our advance man, had picked up for us in Grand Forks. We all got our yuks out of that."

The Laker family is more than players, coaches and management. It has been larger than even Vern realized. Dean Belbas of Palm Desert, California, a former General Mills executive, was the official scorer for the 1958-59 and 1959-60 seasons. He and many others like him behind the scenes are also a part of the family. "I was literally pulled out of the stands halfway through the 1957-58 season and asked if I would be scorer," Belbas recently reminisced. "I said that I would if Jim Weaver, a friend from the University of South Dakota, could do the statistics. They said it was OK, so we worked the table from then until the team left for California."

"In 1958-59, his last season, Vern was still the man who took on the toughest opponent for any team and held his own," Belbas continued. "From the beginning of his career to the end, one trait stood out. He was the ultimate strong rebounder. In the semifinals his last season, we beat St. Louis, which was a young and good team, to move into the championship against the Celtics. Nobody had anticipated for a second that the Lakers would do that well. Once I remember that the Lakers were thinking about drafting Jerry West and also Darrall Imhoff of California. Hot Rod Hundley called West from my apartment and the Lakers went from there.

One thing that happened during Vern's career was that he made an offensive weapon out of a two-handed overhead set shot that nobody thought he would master."

A significant change in the Lakers, along with the rest of the NBA, was the addition of African-American players. "Bob Williams was our first," said Vern, "during the 1955-56 season." Williams played in college at Florida A&M. After a season there, he played in the Air Force. He saw action in twenty Laker games in 1955-56 and four games the next season as Walter Dukes came to the team from the Knicks in a trade for Martin. Ed Fleming, Boo Ellis, and Elgin Baylor continued the progression. "I enjoyed their coming in," said Mikkelsen.

"One of my pro basketball regrets was that I never got to play with my friend 'Sweets', Sweetwater Clifton," Vern said. "But we enjoyed lots of battles against each other after he joined the Knicks [at age 28] in 1950. He called me 'Honey.' I soon learned that he called almost everybody that. One thing he told me was not to complain about train travel until I've tried bus rides like the Globetrotters took."

Mikan and Mikkelsen enjoyed a Harlem Globetrotter television presentation early in 2005. "But we both wished more attention had been paid to the games when we won," Vern said. "After they beat us twice, we beat the Trotters six times in a row." Indeed the Lakes won once in 1949 before Mikkelsen joined the team. Minneapolis won again twice in 1950, and once each in 1951 and 52. The final Laker victory was 103-90 in 1958 as the series concluded.

Also, the entire Minnesota Intercollegiate Athletic Conference proudly watched Hamline grad Mikkelsen advance the league's reputation with his success in the NBA. Serendipity was not the exclusive property of Mikkelsen, of course. Ade

Christenson, who experienced positive celebrity for guiding St. Olaf to six MIAC football championships, was almost into his car to chase a career in medicine when lightning struck. A friend told him a high school coaching job was open at Story City, Iowa. Such opportunities were rare in those Depression days. He got the job, believed God had directed him there, then began spinning out title teams in high school ranks until called to his alma mater St. Olaf to coach in 1927. He also ran the Ole's athletic department for years. His 1958 book, *Verdict of the Scoreboard*, became a primer for those entering the coaching field. There was an emphasis on the value of faith in God that Mikkelsen also promoted. "Having the MIAC guys behind me was important to me," Mikkelsen said.

There was another family that Laker players were seldom aware of, Mikkelsen probably more so than others because of his outgoing personality. His friendship with Pastor David Valen attests to that. Sam Odell of Cave Creek, Arizona, a man unknown to any Laker, is a certain family member because of his devotion, even many years past, to the team and what it stood for. At the time of George Mikan's death, Odell said when interviewed, "I spent some of my growing up years idolizing the Lakers, particularly Mikan and Mikkelsen. While at Gustavus, I played under Coach Tootie Lindberg with a team that faced Vern's Hamline bunch. While I was at Gustavus the Lakers came down to scrimmage us. Mikan and Mikkelsen may be the biggest two reasons I always knew that I would some day get into coaching." And he did, on the community college level in the Phoenix area. He's another preacher's kid, his father having been associated with the Lutheran Bible Institute in Minneapolis. Sam went to high school at Luther Academy in Wahoo, Nebraska, before attending Gustavus.

Chad Coole of Sun Lakes, Arizona, took note at the time of Mikan's death of the effort by Mikkelsen and Mikan to bring—at long last—decent pension and medical benefits to the NBA players who ended their competition in the league before 1965. In a letter to the editor of the *Arizona Republic*, Coole wrote, "Commissioner David Stern…in my opinion… is embarrassed [at] their neglect of these old NBA veterans. Adding insult to injury, once the old vet dies, the pension benefit is reduced by 50 percent to his surviving spouse. If a few of today's overpaid stars got together and showed that they cared about the plight of the few remaining old vets and their wives, this insult would be corrected overnight. These

Mikan and Shaq, 2002

men and their wives… deserve dignity and respect." Men such as Mikan and Mikkelsen have unknowingly recruited a multitude of followers, like Coole and Odell. Charles Barkley spoke for several players and ex-players when he said, "We really need to do something for these guys." Mikkelsen said, "The NBA is just, it seems, waiting until we all die off." Such men, and such talk, comes from a family-like setting.

Finally, there is the sense of ongoing family that exists between the Lakers of old in Minneapolis and the world-renowned Lakers of the last forty-five years in Los Angeles.

The original Lakers represented a work of art that was painted by rank amateurs. There were, in ownership positions, an Ice Capades promoter named Morris Chalfen and a movie-theater magnate, Ben Berger. To run the club, they convinced the owner of the 620 Club, a Hennepin Avenue restaurant that featured roast turkey, to buy in also. He was Max Winter, best known in years previous in the Twin Cities as a manager of fighters. He went into the ring with some shrewd promoters in basketball as well as boxing.

When Mikkelsen stepped into a position of prominence with the early Lakers, he had developed two personal sports characteristics. For him, "fun" was in winning, after a battle for supremacy on a basketball court. The thrill was in making winning a habit the way they did.

Mik gave scant consideration to the lucre involved. Indeed, from start to finish of his pro basketball career he can scarcely remember any negotiation of a salary figure. As to rewards of material value, Vern has to test his memory. "When I was a senior in high school, I was at an event of some kind in Minneapolis for basketball players from different towns. We all received a medallion of some type. It seemed huge to me then. It is tucked away to this day with the mementos of my athletic career that my mom saved.

"When we won the national small-college tournament in Kansas City, we each received a gold basketball inlaid with diamonds. I received an all-tournament team watch, a very fancy one, much like the Bulova watch I received for being named most-valuable player at the Los Angeles Invitational earlier that season. I wore them alternately for years. Then, Jean had them cleaned up and gave one to each of the boys, Tom and John."

That was it for ornamental jewelry in high school and at Hamline, although each player received a trophy when they won the NAIA title at Kansas City.

During the time Mikkelsen played professionally, athletes, be it in basketball, football or baseball, never played "for the ring" as they do now.

"I did receive a beautiful clock from my teammates after my last game, as Jean and my parents stood on the court with me." Halsey Hall, who covered the retirement story for the *Minneapolis Star*, quoted Mikkelsen as telling the crowd: "A clock from my teammates! I had thought they would make it a calendar." At that time, Halsey referred to Vern as "the balding blond from Askov."

As mentioned in the introduction, the Los Angeles Lakers honored Coach Kundla, Mikkelsen, Mikan, and other ex-Minneapolis players at the Staples Center on April 11, 2002. Arilee Pollard represented her late husband. Each of the Minneapolis elder-stars was later sent a huge diamond-encrusted ring identical to the ones the 2002 NBA champion Lakers of Los Angeles had received. The huge rings were appraised at $10,000 but national collectors were immediately offering almost twice that much for them. Whatever the monetary worth, "it's something I'd never part with, regardless of the offer," Mik said.

Charles Stenvig, former mayor of Minneapolis and a 100 percent Norwegian, suggested that another Mikkelsen family existed. "The whole of northern Europe, Scandinavia, is part of the Mikkelsen story," he said.

Another element of family in the Mikkelsen story involves the Minnesota Timberwolves of the Kevin Garnett era. One of Vern's father's best friends was Otto Hoiberg, who introduced a young Mikkelsen to the game of basketball in Askov in 1939. Otto's grandson, Fred Hoiberg, later developed a friendship with Vern, as they happened to live only a few miles apart, Hoiberg in Chaska, Minnesota, and Vern in the Minnetonka area. Fred eventually became one of the most accurate three-point shooters in the NBA. "I got to know Fred's dad, Eric, who taught in Ames. I also watched as Fred became not only an excellent shooter for the Timberwolves, but one of the best total players in the game—defense, passing, and intelligence were as much a part of his game as shooting." Fred told Vern, "I've been picking people's brains about the game in my twelve years in the league."

"Not only do I admire his game," Vern said, "but I like Fred as a young man, good father, good son." During the 2004-05 season the 6-foot-5 Hoiberg led the NBA in three-point accuracy with 48.3%, but the following summer he had serious medical problems caused by an aneurysm, and it ended his basketball-playing career. He had open-heart surgery in June of 2005 and was fitted with a pacemaker. He had been diagnosed as having an aortic valve difficulty in college at Iowa State, though it was not regarded as serious. The test which detects heart issues most thoroughly, an echocardiogram, is now done by several NBA teams. Hoiberg believes it should be done by all of them. (It is given to outstanding prospects in pre-draft camp.)

Although he didn't know it at the time, Mikkelsen was developing another kinship when he visited hospitals in the Twin Cities to chat with folks undergoing medical difficulties of one kind or another. On one such visit, Mikkelsen spent considerable time at the Minneapolis Veterans Administration Hospital. While there he assured Arnold DeJong of Orange City, Iowa, that he would battle back successfully from a series of hip operations. Vern had no idea that he'd have considerable hip problems of his own in a few years.

14

Life without Jean (and George)

Vern Mikkelsen, civilian, endured two crushing blows in the two and a half years between December 19, 2002, and June 2, 2005. His wife of forty-seven years, Jean Mikkelsen, died six days before Christmas in 2002 after agonizing lingering illnesses. She was seventy-two. And George Mikan's death in 2005 brought to an end a friendship of both basketball and family that had continued to strengthen during the big center's final years of battling diabetes and kidney failure. Mikan lost a leg and other parts of his body to diabetes and endured almost five hours of dialysis every Monday, Wednesday, and Friday during the last ten years of his life.

As Vern weathered these two tragedies, particularly the days just prior to and following each of the two funeral services, his mind often lingered over thoughts of better times.

Vern has been asked about the value of basketball in absorbing the lessons of life. To which he responds, "That goes both ways. Yes, I am sure that my years of playing basketball, twenty wonderful years all told, did influence my other life, the one off the court. But values instilled in me by my parents and men like Otto Hoiberg and Joe Hutton were reflected in the dedication that I had for the playing of the game of basketball itself."

When Vern reminisced about how young he was—sixteen—when he invaded the Hamline campus, one of his best basketball friends always came to mind. Jim Pollard was only seventeen when he graduated from Oakland Tech High School in January of 1940, leaving his high-school team in mid-season. Within a few days he was wearing the uniform of the Oakland Golden State Creamery, having moved almost immediately into the most testing brand of independent competition as a player in the American Basketball League.

"Pollard was an inspiration to me in so many ways," Mikkelsen said. "In games, for example, he dominated his opponent on both ends of the court. He could have been known simply for his amazing grace while dunking a basketball, as he did often in practice just to entertain us. But like so many of his peers, he believed the dunk to be not only a hot dog play, but embarrassing to an opponent. He would not do it in games, content simply to fly and then finger-roll the basketball into the net. In many ways, Jim reminded me of my Hamline mentor and friend Howie Schultz. Pollard certainly could have played organized baseball had he headed in that direction. He was a marvelous pitcher, spending many a Sunday with the Jordan, Minnesota, team in a fast brand of amateur baseball. Howie and Jim each had a fierce yet quiet competitive spirit, demanding the best of themselves and of those they played with—including me. Many's the time Jim and I would privately discuss after a game moments when I could have done this or that in addition to what else I had done. I valued both those friendships and learned, in different ways, how better to play the game. Also, away from the basketball of the day, Howie would talk to me about Jackie Robinson's breakthrough into the Dodger lineup, and what Jackie went through. Pollard was aware of Robinson's success from the time Jackie was a football, basketball, track, and baseball standout at UCLA."

Pollard and Mikkelsen talked often as roommates with the Lakers on the road starting with Mik's third season. Pollard also liked the words that came out of the West Coast about two athletes who could simply fly—himself and Robinson.

Schultz confided in Mikkelsen some of the insults Robinson had to listen to in breaking the color line. Howie asked the Brooklyn teammate and foe, after Schultz was dealt to the Phillies, how Jackie could possibly endure the profanation sent his way. Vern said that Jackie just assured Howie that his (Robinson's) day would come. No argument there.

There was a bit of Lutheranism in the Mikkelsen-Schultz relationship as well. Schultz' early baseball came on a field next to St. Stephen Church (German Lutheran) in a day-school setting. Howie was older, but grew up in the same Wilson High School neighborhood near Hamline that many of Vern's friends did.

Coach Hutton seemed to know that Mikkelsen would succeed in professional basketball. But become the sixth player in NBA history to score 10,000 points? Certainly not. That Mik would be the most successful of the six players Hutton sent into the pros in the seven years between 1943 and 1950? Well, maybe. That Mikkelsen would join Mikan and Pollard to form the most respected Big Three until Wilt and pals at Philadelphia, or perhaps ever? Certainly not.

Might Coach Hutton have suspected that Vern, despite his aggressiveness on the court, would develop a reputation off the court for congeniality? Probably. And then, as the big guy turned away to resume life after Coach Joe, his smile broadened with the realization that the Rutabaga Kid out of Askov had been reunited with his coach in a final, unique way. Hutton's last summers were spent satisfying himself with the task of raising carrots, a relative of the rutabaga.

The death of his wife Jean after more than forty-seven years of marriage—"a pairing made in heaven" Vern always said— brought a different kind of grieving into Mikkelsen's life. He had been a dedicated and loving care-giver for Jean during her last five years in their antique-filled home. She was interred in the northwest corner of Groveland Cemetery just a few blocks from their home. Looking east from her burial plot one can gaze at the Minneapolis skyline in the distance. "Tom, John, and I and her host of good friends and family members miss her very much to this day, and I'm sure we always will," Vern said. Among all of the words of condolence the Mikkelsens received upon Jean's death, one message was of particular consequence to them: Twin Cities media giant Sid Hartman, out of town the day of Jean's funeral, "made special effort to get to us a lovely card and thoughtful letter," Vern said. Mikkelsen had known Sid since Hamline basketball days.

Vern's reverie at that time centered on the joy he and Jean had shared. "One of the most-significant moments was when John Kundla and I entered the Basketball Hall of Fame together, along with such impressive names as Kareem Abdul-Jabbar and Cheryl Miller.

"Jean and the boys sat there beaming as I worked my way through my acceptance speech, one that she had heard me practicing for weeks. She smiled broadly before I went up front to speak. Answering questions as to preparation, I replied, 'It ought to be OK. I've been working on it for 14 years.' George first nominated me in 1979.

"Jean had heard me say the words many times, so she expected it when I said that I was accepting the Hall of Fame honor on behalf of all power forwards, many of whom played in relative obscurity but incurred the same bruises.

Jean ca 1998

"Jean told me that her eyes were even more misty than mine when I choked up at the end in saying I owed it all to family, friends, and faith. I hope no one thought it disrespectful in any way when I spoke of the names on the list of Hall of Famers. I said that alphabetically. I had had some association with about 70 percent of them, starting with Paul Arizin and Red Auerbach then, as examples, Clair Bee, and Elgin [Baylor], Bob Cousy, and so on. I could have gone on to Bob Davies of the old Royals and through the others one by one. I have a deep appreciation of basketball history. Four years later, when I looked at an updated list, there at the alphabetical end was Minnesota's own Fred Zollner. That made it A to Z."

Toward the end of Jean's service at Gethsemane Lutheran Church in Hopkins, not far from the route sons Tom and John traveled to get to high school, Vern's musing took him to a near tragedy that occurred on January 17, 1960. That snowy night, with Mikkelsen retired from basketball and just getting a good start in his Northwestern Agency insurance business, and Mikan running his travel business, the Lakers' DC-3 bringing the team home from a game in St. Louis was nowhere to be found. It had drifted off course in a snowstorm that took away its electrical power, thus silencing the radio and guidance gear. "The minute I heard about it early that following morning," Vern said. "My fear was immediate for Jim Pollard, who had taken over as coach midway through that final season in Minneapolis. Fortunately the pilot was able to land the plane in a snow-covered cornfield outside Carroll, Iowa. Scared but safe is how Jim described their feelings as they got out of the plane. Jim said the pilot, Vern Ullman, had to stick his head out of a window at his side to see anything because the windshield had frosted over. They say people still stop in Carroll and ask where the Laker plane went down. Yep, a tourist attraction."

Jean always was an effective sounding board for her husband's stories, the ones he would use to amuse those who took the game of basketball too seriously. One of her favorites was the time the Lakers had to rush to the train in their sweat-soaked uniforms [see page 90]. "Jean also liked one in particular that involved Johnny [Kundla]. We used to stop once in a while in Kansas City and listen to an attractive lounge singer named Marian Russell. She was something to see. I'm sure John felt it was beneficial to get our minds off competition once in a while. One night we landed in Kansas City for a day off before heading the next evening to Cincinnati. I think Kundla arranged the stop so the boys could listen to Marian. She was singing at the Phillips Hotel, where we stayed. When we got off the ground in the evening headed for Cincinnati, somebody, I think it was either Hot Rod [Hundley] or Slick [Bob Leonard] had sneaked Marian onto the plane for a little surprise songfest for the rest of the boys. When she came out of the cockpit to surprise us, the guys on the team who thought themselves quite manly and attractive, had their eyes opened wide. She headed straight to the back of the plane where Kundla always sat. 'Now, where is that handsome coach?' she said. I think Johnny was more than a little embarrassed. But a little tickled, too, as she serenaded him instead of the players. And I also think that Marian wasn't just smuggled aboard against her will. I think she might have had a singing gig in Cincinnati and used the guys for free transportation.

"Funny in retrospect what a guy thinks about when he has just lost his dear wife. I can remember Tom and John shooting baskets, carrying the obvious burden of being sons of a college and Laker player like myself. It was impossible to measure up to what people think a son of an athlete must be. George Mikan's kids had the same difficulty to overcome athletically.

"In my case I can remember back in Askov playing hoops on makeshift baskets on garages or in barn haylofts. That experience lead me as an adult into an interesting business venture with athlete and announcer Paul Giel. Throughout the 1950s Paul was a jock like me. Then he went to work for WCCO radio. Our friendship developed further when our kids went to grade school together, and we eventually decided to go into business together selling portable basketball hoops. Around 1970, I was selling these portable, adjustable baskets, and they were moving well with customers. They were very much better than the crude baskets of my boyhood. But though the inventive part of the deal was exceptional, the manufacturing plant went broke. Partner Paul Giel and I had none available for our customers.

"Every once in a while Jean would be looking out the window to the basket at our home and watch as the boys shooting baskets changed to a game of horse, then to one on one, and then to three on three when other fellas showed up. She would say to me, 'Vern, it's getting pretty rough out there.'

Tom, Vern, and John Mikkelsen at a Lakers game in 2004

I would just smile and nod my head, remembering one time when I was at Hamline and my mom visited me, saw a bruised and swollen left eye, and felt sorry for me while wondering what had happened. I tried to explain to her that Coach Hutton thought it best for me, and it sure was in the long run, to get beat up a little bit in practice. And we had two otherwise nice guys who did just that extremely well. Rube Lieske was an ex-Marine out of Franklin, Minnesota, and George Bergwall had been in the Army for the campaign in North Africa. Two very tough guys who were very good at doing what coach requested. Practices in some ways were tougher than games. The time my mom wondered about, George had caught a thumb in my left eye some way and I looked a little the worse for wear." In fact, Mikkelsen lost the sight in his left eye at age fifty.

The home on Willmatt Hill where Vern and Jean raised their two sons was in the western Minneapolis suburb of Hopkins near Lake Minnetonka. "The boys sometimes played sports of all kinds at a place called Excelsior Commons on the lake seven miles from our house," Vern said. "It was right close to there where, before Jean and I got married, I roomed for two years with a dear friend, Einer Anderson. In fact, it was Einer and Rollie Seltz, who each could play the game well, who talked me into playing Sundays with an Excelsior amateur baseball team. They kind of hid me in an outfield spot. But as I said, I was no darn good."

It was the Hamline "family" of friends that helped Vern endure the loss of his beloved Jean. The school, still affiliated with the Methodist church, had an enrollment of about 1,200 when Vern attended in the late 1940s. "I couldn't believe how many of them sent expressions of sympathy," Mikkelsen said. In 2005, Hamline's enrollment of undergraduate students numbered 1,800. "When I got to Hamline in the fall of 1945," Mikkelsen said, "I learned something immediately. I may have been the biggest and clumsiest of the new students, but others were just as raw in many ways as I was. I fell in with a wonderful group of guys, close friends to this day. Gordy Walker, Einer Anderson, Walt Lee, Sam Richie, Carl Miller, Hap Holmgren, Keith Paisley, Supe Lundsten, Tom Purcell and Joe Jr. were pals growing up. Almost all of them lived in the neighborhood surrounding the school. Adding myself, and a few others, we became a campus softball and volleyball team called the Potlikkers. Actually, it was a name they had called themselves as kids. We had similar interests, enjoyed each other's company. I thought that was something, me being a country boy and them from the big city of St. Paul. Important subjects, like girls—I was dating a girl named Jean Olson at the time—were discussed regularly."

Jean and Vern's older son, Thomas Verner, moved to Phoenix with his wife Jennifer in 2001. The couple had met in Los Angeles years earlier while both were working in the movie industry, and they were married in Mendocino, California, a small coastal town 105 miles north of San Francisco on the ruggedly beautiful coast of the Pacific Ocean. The reception was held at a private condo complex named "Jean's Vista." By coincidence? Vern will tell you there are no coincidences.

Vern's other son, John, is single, and lives in Minneapolis, "and is a great help to me," Mik said. "I'm still his father and he's still my son, but more importantly, we've also become best friends."

George Mikan moved to Scottsdale, Arizona in 1999 after his lower right leg was lost to diabetes. Thereafter, and increasingly following son Tom's moving his family to Phoenix, Mikkelsen regularly visited the Valley of the Sun. "George and I were teammates, yes," Mik said, "but much more than that, we were the closest of friends for fifty years. We talked often on the phone. And after I started visiting Phoenix a few times a year, we would get together at his Grayhawk home and laugh about many of the things that happened to us and for us through the years. And, oh yes, we would cry together on occasion, too. His dear wife Pat would be there with us, hearing some of the stories for the umpteenth time, I'm sure, laughing with us and drying her eyes often.

"When I retired in 1959," Vern recalled recently, "George told me that one of the greatest benefits would be that I could enjoy those special family gatherings for holidays. My wife

Vern and George Mikan at the piano during the Laker years

Jean certainly agreed. That's why I choke up every time I hear George's son Terry tell how George offered the same toast at every family gathering after grace was said before a meal —'Here's to kindness'."

"George, devotedly Catholic, loved to hear me tell of all of the Scandinavian influences on my life—starting of course with my Danish Lutheranism led by my dad, the pastor. George heard all about the church in which Jean and I were married. It was at a Lutheran Bible Camp near Spicer and the building itself was a replica of a famous Stave Kirche in Norway. George and I would recall how we got out of the limelight for lunch often, especially during our ABA management days, at the Monte Carlo Restaurant at Third Street and Washington Avenue.

"Another of our favorites involved a leather-lunged spectator one night at Madison Square Garden. Whoever had put the stuff together for inclusion in that evening's program had included the fact that during my college years I had sung in an operetta with the Hamline choir. That night, just as time expired, I was fouled. As I stood in deafening silence at the free throw line, a Knicks fan bellowed down from the nickel seats, 'Mikkelsen! You should have stuck with opera!' I missed both freethrows and we lost the game."

There was the time that New York Giants football coach Allie Sherman looked Vern over when the Lakers were playing the Knicks. Seeing that 6-foot-7, 235-pound body of Mikkelsen mix it up at one end of the floor and race to the other end for more of the same impressed Sherman. "He offered me what I was making with the Lakers if I had a successful tryout with the Giants. Naturally, I said I had no interest. Mikan ribbed me about it when he found out."

Mikan and Mikkelsen laughed, too, at the memory of the two of them, along with Jim Pollard, doing their "looking up" trick at Times Square. Here would be these three giants all making a production of seeing something unusual as they gazed excitedly up into the higher reaches of the surrounding buildings. Soon a whole group of New Yorkers or visitors would be staring up into the sky. "At nothing," Mikkelsen would say with a chuckle.

"Then, too, there was the Swedish influence provided mostly by Jean," Mikkelsen said. "After we had lived for a while in the first home we built on Willmatt Hill, the developer told us the lot right next to us would be sold. We bought it and under Jean's direction we had constructed for us an almost exact copy of one of our favorite places to visit in Sweden. Selma Lagerlöf won the Nobel Prize in Literature in 1909. She had written, among other things, a book I devoured as a kid, *The Wonderful Adventures of Nils*. She had lived in a beautiful Swedish farmhouse a hundred miles from Stockholm which Jean and I traveled to often. Jean simply loved it, especially the way it caught the setting sun on its light yellow sides. Well, under Jean's rapt direction, a contractor matched it almost foot for foot on the new lot, next to our first home. George would sit patiently and let me tell that tale time after time, smiling all the while."

The diabetes which eventually struck down Mikan, along with kidney failure, landed on Vern in 1996. "They caught mine much earlier than they did George's," Mikkelsen said. "So as he was mentioning the destruction it had ravaged on him [something he seldom did, by the way], he told me to keep praying and to keep following doctor's orders as to diet and medication. I have been pretty faithful doing that. Actually, it had been Jean who had been observing me as I became more and more occupied with sweet treats. She urged me to get my sugar count checked. Which I did. Learned of my situation. And have been almost as good about minding instructions as I would have had to be with Jean around."

When Mikkelsen finally decided in 1993 that constant pain in his left hip had become more than he could bear, he received a new one. At about the same time, in typical brother to brother fashion, John Kundla was facing the same obstacle. "My first one just didn't work," Vern said. "Three years later I had it redone. It's still not right, but they've tried to make it work. I'm relatively OK now with the use of a twenty-four-hour support brace. Also, they made for me a cowhide special swimming pool brace that really helps me exercise the hip.

John has had two hip replacements on one side and one on the other. Like me, he does OK. But to see the two of us ambling along on our canes must be something."

While in the recovery stage from his original hip replacement, Vern occupied himself with a new heart-driven task. Hamline had fallen out of touch with many of its Mikkelsen-era (and later) athletes. Dan Loritz, vice president for university relations, was determined to do something about it. Loritz spoke of the challenge with Glenn Gumlia, who had been a member of the Pipers' 1942 small-college championship team. Gumlia recommended Vern as someone who could assist in such a project. Loritz and Mikkelsen then joined minds in an effort, as Loritz said, to "build trust again between some of our past athletes and the school. Vern was the catalyst as we made that happen. He solidified the effort by being a personal ambassador to a large group of alumni." What resulted was a $100 million fund-raising success between 1993 and 2004.

Among the alumni who returned to the campus often for various events was 1957 graduate Jack Schmid of Kansas City. He said, "I got to Hamline because as a kid in Springfield, Minnesota, I followed what Hamline, and Vern, did in basketball. I wanted to be part of it, so I went to Hamline and tried out for basketball as a walk-on. Another reason for my attending Hamline was that my sister Mary went there and was a choir member along with Vern for one year. To further the Schmid-Mikkelsen relationship, my sister eventually married Jim Holstein out of the University of Cincinnati. He was a Laker teammate of Vern's for four seasons starting in 1952-53. Jim played Western Minny baseball for Springfield and life-guarded at the municipal pool which was managed summers by my sister."

When George Mikan was dying, Vern felt closer and closer to George's widow, Pat, because of what he had gone through while his own spouse, Jean, was struggling to stay alive. "She was so strong, especially for just a little woman. Pat was as short as George was tall. Yet both were symbolic of the strength available through love and faith," Vern said.

Another favorite reminiscence of the two then-aging ex-Laker stars dealt with their time with the short-lived ABA, George as commissioner and Vern in his role of general manager of the Muskies-Pipers. "Whenever something unusual would come up that I felt I needed the commissioner's advice on, I had difficulty contacting George," Mikkelsen said. "He was busy putting out fires all over the place. We had lots of problems financially, of course, because we couldn't attract enough paying customers. The old Metropolitan Sports Arena in Bloomington where we played took the ticket-window money before we ever saw what there was of it.

Mikkelsen spoke at both of Mikan's memorial tributes. The first was shortly after George's death in Scottsdale. The second was on July 31, 2005, in the lobby of the Target Center in Minneapolis.

"I sat with Bill Russell at George Mikan's Scottsdale memorial service in June of 2005. Bill Sharman, who also was a good friend of George, was there, too. All three of us were extremely close to Big George and enjoyed each other's company also. I was extremely pleased that I was asked, with them, to speak. I tried to make my words light and positive because I knew George would want it that way."

The Target Center event was organized by Dennis Schulstad, the same businessman who had been instrumental in raising funds for the nine-foot statue of Mikan that stands in that particular lobby today.

The Mikan statue was dedicated on April 8, 2001. With Mikkelsen assisting Schulstad, the statue-raising had a gigantic side benefit. Money raised to complete the project exceeded by about $500,000 what was required. And, as the two had planned and announced, that sum went to the Maxi Fund for Juvenile Diabetes, originated by former Green Bay Packer Max McGee and based in Appleton, Wisconsin.

At the two Mikan memorials, as with his wife Jean's funeral and Joe Hutton's, Mik found time to reminisce. There were moments of sadness in his reverie, to be sure, but far more were the occasions that a smile would cross his face. An example was when he remembered his fright when speaking as a college student to youngsters attending the German Lutheran church at Good Thunder, Minnesota. Rollie Seltz' father was pastor there.

One of the frustrating moments was when he considered just how little progress had been made on a special request made to the NBA and its current players by himself and Mikan. "Way back in 1952," Mikkelsen said, "Bob Cousy and I were appointed to do interviews, Bob in the East and me in the West, of players of that era to see what kind of a push we could make for decent pensions and medical benefits. More than fifty-three years later, with the same proposal only now much more urgent, George and I seemed to make no more gains than Bob and I had a half century earlier for the pre-1965 guys."

Mikkelsen assured himself again that he was "the luckiest basketball player ever because I got in there with Pollard and Mikan. One, George, voted the outstanding basketball player of the first half of the twentieth century. And Pollard, who died in 1993, recognized throughout the pro game's inner circle, the players, as the most gifted player of his time. That was probably true at least up to Michael Jordan.

"I heard once that an honor that slipped away from Jim, as others may have, took place in 1954. The NBA All-Star Game was in New York City. I was lucky to play in it also. Almost at game's end, so reported Marc Spears, who covered the game for the *Denver Post*, a vote was taken on the game's most-valuable player. Jim Pollard was voted the honor, the vote having been taken just before the end of regulation time. Well, George made two free throws at the buzzer and it went into overtime. Cousy scored ten of the East's fourteen points as they won in overtime. Another vote was taken and this time Cousy won.

"There was no question that a portion of Pollard's star was in George's shadow because they were on the same team. They simply were the two best of their era. I read someplace that when the three of us scored 65 percent of the Laker points in 1950-51, it was the best of all time except for 67 percent by Chamberlain and his front-line partners in 1962." Of course, Wilt averaged better than 50 points a game himself.

"At George's memorial service in Scottsdale, I sat with Bill Sharman and Bill Russell," Mikkelsen said one day in August of 2005 while reminiscing in his Minnetonka town-house loft office. Sharman once played baseball for the St. Paul Saints, getting to know Mikan and Vern then. "Whenever I see Bill Russell, one of the kindest men I've known, I remember how the Celtics of his day would funnel the opponents' offense to him in a shot-blocking role in the lane. Our approach was similar I guess. George, Jim, and I would be deep while playing against our assigned opponents. That allowed Martin, or Harrison, or Ferrin, or whoever to gamble a bit out front going for steals with the assurance if somebody got loose in the direction of the basket he would have us to deal with." The Men of Steel made for the Men of Steal.

The Big Three were also similarly avid in their pursuit of educational objectives. Mikan wound up with a law degree,

Mikkelsen with a master's in psychology, and Pollard would not quit until he had earned his degree in education from the University of Minnesota in 1953. He then practice-taught at Minneapolis Washburn, as did Mikkelsen.

Mikkelsen was constantly aware of the God-created factors in his life. Many are obvious. But how about these? Howie Schultz was an

Vern's basketball card, ca 1958

eighth of an inch taller than the armed-service maximum of the time, 6-foot-6. That left him available in the fall of 1945 to tutor the kid from Askov. Height seems often to be governed by heredity. Vern's dad was 6-foot-2, his sister Hertha 6-foot-1, his sister Esther 5-foot-10 and his mother 5-foot-9. No surprise that Vern reached 6-foot-7. His sons Tom and John are 6-3 and 6-6, respectively. Height not withstanding, Mikkelsen always had faith that God made his fate "inescapable." When it comes to the value of being as tall as he is, "or as tall as my boys might become, was never talked about in my family," Vern said.

Not one to question past decisions, Mik has been able to smile about the loss of a fortune—twenty-five percent of the

Vern with Askov classmates Jim Pearson and
Glen "Buzz" Mortensen at the Askov Rutabaga Festival, 1995
(see photo on page 15)

$5.2 million Bob Short received when selling the Lakers to
Jack Kent Cooke. And if something had happened to keep
Vern in the mix, Cooke later sold the team to Jerry Buss for
10 times that.

Yet for Mikkelsen fulfillment came from benefits other
than money. His salary topped at $25,000 in his final year.
Mikan reached $35,000 in his prime ("close to forty thou-
sand with side deals," Vern said). Mikkelsen, in Minnesota
at least, killed the supposition that only the city kid could
play basketball beyond high school. He brought country into
those collisions under the NBA baskets, grabbing rebounds
and accumulating fouls at record rates. ("Kundla would never take me out.") Mikkelsen called his game "bruising, not

smooth." The Laker trio lured elderly spectators, including women, to games that formerly had been frequented almost exclusively by cigar- and cigarette-smoking males. The rowdyism of the 1930s and early '40s seemed to diminish in games involving the Lakers.

The blow to Minneapolis when the Lakers departed for California was softened with the 1961 arrival of the Twins and Vikings. Fans tended to remember the team fondly rather than with rancor. Still, there were those who blamed the Lakers for the Gophers' football difficulties after 1960. "They said we influenced big kids to go into basketball rather than football," Vern said with a grin.

Is Mikkelsen in danger of falling into obscurity? In August of 2005 he received a request for autographed photos to be presented to five boys making Eagle Scout in Chino, California. "The boys are big basketball fans," wrote Scout leader Taylor Bladh when making the request.

Vern still receives mail and autograph requests from fans worldwide. In 2006, the Fleer Sports Card Company produced a special Vern Mikkelsen Card and Vern signed 400 of them for surprise placement in the packs of NBA collectors cards that Fleer distributes commercially all over the world.

Vern says, "It's still nice to be remembered."

Index